Firebase Cookbook

Over 70 recipes to help you create real-time web and mobile applications with Firebase

Houssem Yahiaoui

BIRMINGHAM - MUMBAI

Firebase Cookbook

First published: November 2017

Production reference: 1281117

Published by Packt Publishing Ltd.
Livery Place
35 Livery Street
Birmingham
B3 2PB, UK.

ISBN 978-1-78829-633-5

www.packtpub.com

Credits

Author
Houssem Yahiaoui

Reviewer
Thomas David Kehoe

Commissioning Editor
Kunal Chaudhari

Acquisition Editor
Larissa Pinto

Content Development Editor
Aditi Gour

Technical Editor
Sushmeeta Jena

Copy Editor
Safis Editing

Project Coordinator
Devanshi Doshi

Proofreader
Safis Editing

Indexer
Francy Puthiry

Graphics
Jason Monteiro

Production Coordinator
Deepika Naik

About the Author

Houssem Yahiaoui, a backend engineer at Xapo from Algeria, has almost 4 years, experience in building everything from backend services to mobile apps using Hybrid, Not so Hybrid and Native Approaches. Houssem is also a Telerik Developer Expert title holder and community power believer. He's also a Google Developer Group Lead Organizer, Algeria Tech Community (Community Manager), and speaker at numerous national and international events from DevFests to DroidCon, sharing his experience of web technologies, and a love for serverless approaches and Firebase.

About the Reviewer

Thomas David Kehoe makes technology for speech clinics to treat stuttering and other speech disorders. He is interested in how auditory processing affects second language acquisition. He develops web apps using Firebase, Angular, and JavaScript.

www.PacktPub.com

For support files and downloads related to your book, please visit www.PacktPub.com. Did you know that Packt offers eBook versions of every book published, with PDF and ePub files available? You can upgrade to the eBook version at www.PacktPub.com and as a print book customer, you are entitled to a discount on the eBook copy. Get in touch with us at service@packtpub.com for more details.

At www.PacktPub.com, you can also read a collection of free technical articles, sign up for a range of free newsletters and receive exclusive discounts and offers on Packt books and eBooks.

https://www.packtpub.com/mapt

Get the most in-demand software skills with Mapt. Mapt gives you full access to all Packt books and video courses, as well as industry-leading tools to help you plan your personal development and advance your career.

Why subscribe?

- Fully searchable across every book published by Packt
- Copy and paste, print, and bookmark content
- On demand and accessible via a web browser

Customer Feedback

Thanks for purchasing this Packt book. At Packt, quality is at the heart of our editorial process. To help us improve, please leave us an honest review on this book's Amazon page at `www.amazon.in/dp/1788296338`.

If you'd like to join our team of regular reviewers, you can email us at `customerreviews@packtpub.com`. We award our regular reviewers with free eBooks and videos in exchange for their valuable feedback. Help us be relentless in improving our products!

Table of Contents

Preface

Introduction

Whether we like it or not, the world is moving toward different development schemes in ways that technically differ from one team to another or even from one developer to another. As a backend developer, I understand the hustle, from having a really dependable database to implementing an effective authentication system that can be relied on to keep things secure, without forgetting about the authorization part, where you simply manage the part of who has access to what.

Such a hustle is not even the beginning; in a mobile-first world, improving your users' mobile application functionalities is a critical task because you will always need to improve your application security, maintain a notification system that scales, and have a great user interface and experience, but even with all this, you will the analytics, revenue generation part which is still essential, because you simply want to listen to your users' needs and breaking point within your application in easy seamless way without too much pain.

Firebase provides all of that and much more in a set of interconnected products that simply lets your application have everything that Firebase has to offer. This book will go through each topic over the 13 chapters divided into problem/solution recipes. All the points covered here come from real-world scenarios that each and every new or old application might have faced or will face within its development workflow.

What this book covers

Chapter 1, *Firebase - Getting Started*, begins with the process of integrating Firebase and its services into different platforms and environments, from frontend and backend projects to Android/iOS projects.

Chapter 2, *Firebase Real-Time Database*, introduces one of the most used features of Firebase—Firebase Real Time. It covers how to implement the daily input entering and retrieval and update of your data; it also covers how we can structure our data better and finishes by enabling all these features and enabling them offline.

Chapter 3, *File Management with Firebase Storage*, explains how we can upload, download, and manage files within our Firebase Storage.

`Chapter 4`, *Firebase Authentication*, presents the different ways in which you can authenticate your users using Firebase, from traditional authentication to an OAuth-based login process that is different from Facebook, Google, and Twitter.

`Chapter 5`, *Securing Application Flow with Firebase Rules*, explains how to secure Firebase Database and Firebase Storage using the powerful Firebase authorization rules.

`Chapter 6`, *Progressive Applications Powered by Firebase*, shows how to turn a boring application with old features into a progressive one using service workers and Firebase.

`Chapter 7`, *Firebase Admin SDK*, describes how we can create a basic dashboard and interact with other Firebase functionalities from the diverse set with more authorization and a more powerful API to manage users and notifications.

`Chapter 8`, *Extend Firebase with Cloud Functions*, covers how we can use Firebase Cloud Functions and integrate it and interact with different Firebase products to extend its functionalities and go literally serverless ending up with deployment interactivity within the Firebase console.

`Chapter 9`, *We're Done, Let's Deploy*, is about deploying your code to the Firebase Static hosting and making some config-based customizations to the user experience.

`Chapter 10`, *Integrating Firebase with NativeScript*, shows the proper way to use Firebase within the NativeScript a lot of platforms applications.

`Chapter 11`, *Integrating Firebase with Android/iOS Natively*, is all about implementing Firebase features from Interacting with the Realtime Database to authentication in native context for Android and iOS applications.

`Chapter 12`, *Hack Application's Growth*, dives into the little functionalities that simply generate more leads and improve the application's user experience, covering app invites and topic-based notifications.

`Chapter 13`, *Adding Analytics and Maximizing Earnings*, shows how you can integrate analytics and incorporate AdMob so that you can generate revenue from different ad types.

`Appendix`, *Firebase Cloud FireStore*, talks about the power points of Firebase Cloud Firestore and its differences from earlier model.

What you need for this book

The content requirements are fairly easy for the first 10 chapters; no matter what your operating system or your code editor is, you're always covered.

However, in `Chapter 11`, *Integrating Firebase with Android/iOS Natively*, we'll start developing for mobile, so while you will be perfectly fine with any operating system (macOs, Linux, or Windows) when developing for Android, we will definitely need a macOS-based computer in order to follow along with iOS-based recipes.

Who this book is for

This book is for anyone who wants to use Firebase for their personal/professional projects. As this book covers multiple platforms and different development environments, there's everything for everyone.

The need for this book will simply come from the willingness to know the interesting parts that makes Firebase an interconnected set of tools that simply makes developers' lives much easier by demystifying the hustle that developers usually come across while creating projects from scratch or just implementing new features. So technically, like I mentioned, there's everything for everyone.

Conventions

In this book, you will find a number of text styles that distinguish between different kinds of information. Here are some examples of these styles and an explanation of their meaning.

Code words in text, database table names, folder names, filenames, file extensions, path names, dummy URLs, user input, and Twitter handles are shown as follows: "Finally, we will need to implement the `put()` method."

A block of code is set as follows:

```
//Getting the file reference.
var rootRef = firebase.storage().ref();
var imageRef = rootRef.child('images/<image-name>.
  <image-ext>');
```

New terms and **important words** are shown in bold. Words that you see on the screen, for example, in menus or dialog boxes, appear in the text like this: "We clicked on the **Upload to Firebase** button."

Warnings or important notes appear in a box like this.

Tips and tricks appear like this.

Reader feedback

Feedback from our readers is always welcome. Let us know what you think about this book-what you liked or disliked. Reader feedback is important for us as it helps us develop titles that you will really get the most out of.

To send us general feedback, simply e-mail feedback@packtpub.com, and mention the book's title on the subject of your message.

If there is a topic that you have expertise in and you are interested in either writing or contributing to a book, see our author guide at www.packtpub.com/authors.

Customer support

Now that you are the proud owner of a Packt book, we have a number of things to help you to get the most from your purchase.

Downloading the example code

You can download the example code files for this book from your account at http://www.packtpub.com. If you purchased this book elsewhere, you can visit http://www.packtpub.com/support and register to have the files emailed directly to you.

You can download the code files by following these steps:

1. Log in or register to our website using your email address and password.
2. Hover the mouse pointer on the **SUPPORT** tab at the top.
3. Click on **Code Downloads & Errata**.
4. Enter the name of the book in the **Search** box.
5. Select the book for which you're looking to download the code files.

6. Choose from the drop-down menu where you purchased this book from.
7. Click on **Code Download**.

Once the file is downloaded, please make sure that you unzip or extract the folder using the latest version of:

- WinRAR / 7-Zip for Windows
- Zipeg / iZip / UnRarX for Mac
- 7-Zip / PeaZip for Linux

The code bundle for the book is also hosted on GitHub at `https://github.com/PacktPublishing/Firebase-Cookbook`. We also have other code bundles from our rich catalog of books and videos available at `https://github.com/PacktPublishing/`. Check them out!

Downloading the color images of this book

We also provide you with a PDF file that has color images of the screenshots/diagrams used in this book. The color images will help you better understand the changes in the output. You can download this file from `https://www.packtpub.com/sites/default/files/downloads/FirebaseCookbook_ColorImages.pdf`.

Errata

Although we have taken every care to ensure the accuracy of our content, mistakes do happen. If you find a mistake in one of our books-maybe a mistake in the text or the code we would be grateful if you could report this to us. By doing so, you can save other readers from frustration and help us improve subsequent versions of this book. If you find any errata, please report them by visiting `http://www.packtpub.com/submit-errata`, selecting your book, clicking on the **Errata Submission Form** link, and entering the details of your errata. Once your errata are verified, your submission will be accepted and the errata will be uploaded to our website or added to any list of existing errata under the Errata section of that title.

To view the previously submitted errata, go to `https://www.packtpub.com/books/content/support` and enter the name of the book in the search field. The required information will appear under the **Errata** section.

Piracy

Piracy of copyrighted material on the Internet is an ongoing problem across all media. At Packt, we take the protection of our copyright and licenses very seriously. If you come across any illegal copies of our works in any form on the Internet, please provide us with the location address or website name immediately so that we can pursue a remedy.

Please contact us at `copyright@packtpub.com` with a link to the suspected pirated material.

We appreciate your help in protecting our authors and our ability to bring you valuable content.

Questions

If you have a problem with any aspect of this book, you can contact us at `questions@packtpub.com`, and we will do our best to address the problem.

1
Firebase - Getting Started

In this chapter, we will cover the following recipes:

- Creating your first Firebase app
- Adding Firebase to an existing frontend project
- Integrating Firebase in the backend
- Integrating Firebase in Android applications
- Integrating Firebase in iOS applications

Introduction

With the changing web and mobile scene, finding a suitable solution and technology that suits these climbing, fast needs is a must. From web development to mobile, the way we treat APIs, data, and security, and how we make users feel as engaged as we possibly can, is an urgent matter.

Going from a traditional setup to the cloud leads to many new patterns and architectures. **Backend-as-a-service** (**BaaS**), saves us from tons of useless setup and configuration and makes us think of nothing but our application logic.

Here we are introducing Firebase, a feature-heavy BaaS that will make creating your next awesome project a breeze. It will eliminate many tedious tasks and even manpower and will create your server-side code and give you a more secure, well-built platform that will completely change your thoughts about simplicity and scalability.

So, hold on tight and let's start our journey together by creating our first ever Firebase application.

Creating your first Firebase application

The process of creating a Firebase application is straightforward and mainly visual. This recipe will demonstrate the process of creating a Firebase application from scratch.

How to do it...

1. As mentioned previously, we will use nothing but our clicking superpower and our favorite browser. First, head directly to the Firebase official website: `https://firebase.google.com/`. A screenshot of the website page is as follows (*Figure 1*):

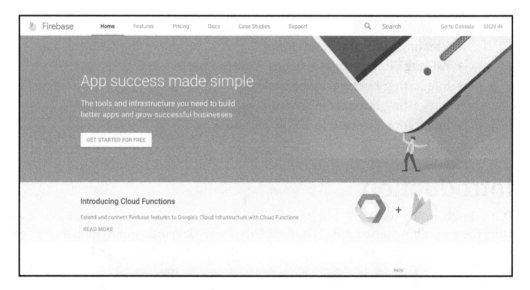

Figure 1: Firebase main screen

2. Now, go to the top navigation bar and click on the **SIGN IN** button. This will lead to another page where you will be introduced to the Google authentication page showcased in the following figure, where you can select the most suitable account for your development work (*Figure 2*):

Figure 2: Firebase - Google authentication

3. Now, after you select the most suitable Google account, you will find yourself redirected to this link: `https://console.firebase.google.com/`. You will find all of your Firebase projects here, and you can introduce new projects as well (*Figure 3*):

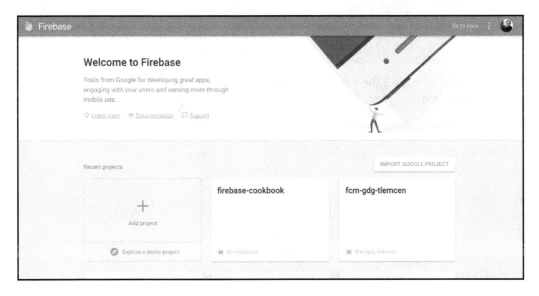

Figure 3: Firebase console

Now, we do have two options: whether to import a Google project or simply start a fresh one. Let us learn how to start a new project.

4. After clicking on the **Add project** plus button, you will be introduced to a model where you can add the **Project name** and **Country/region**. Keep in mind that the **Project name** and **Country** are variables, so you can change their values to the values that suit you best. You can see the page for creating the project in the following screenshot (*Figure 4*):

Figure 4: Firebase project creation

5. After finishing the previous step, you will be redirected to your Firebase dashboard (*Figure 5*):

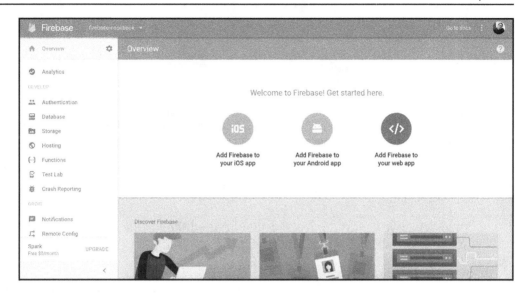

Figure 5: Firebase project dashboard

Congratulations! You've successfully created your first Firebase project. You have seen that the steps are really simple and are applicable to any Firebase project that you may create now or in the future.

Adding Firebase to an existing frontend project

Since Firebase is indeed a backend platform which typically acts as a service, it's not strange to see today's developer ditch the idea of creating a backend in general. They just focus on their frontend, which is actually the main idea behind serverless architecture nowadays.

How to do it...

In order to fully integrate Firebase into our frontend project, which is typically composed of nothing but .html, .css, and .js files, we will need to follow the given steps:

1. Open your favorite code editor and write down the following:

```
<script
    src="https://www.gstatic.com/firebasejs/3.9.0/firebase.js>
</script>
```

```
<script>
    // Initialize Firebase
    // TODO: Replace with your project's customized
     code snippet
    var config = {
        apiKey: "<API_KEY>",
        authDomain: "<PROJECT_ID>.firebaseapp.com",
        databaseURL: "https://<DATABASE_NAME>.firebaseio.com",
        storageBucket: "<BUCKET>.appspot.com",
        messagingSenderId: "<SENDER_ID>",
    };
    firebase.initializeApp(config);
</script>
```

So, what we've just done is simply imported the Firebase core library from its CDN and initialized it with a configuration object that Firebase gave us out of the box.

2. Now, let's grab our pre-filled configuration form our Firebase project dashboard. The steps are actually easy--login to your Firebase project. (*Figure 6*):

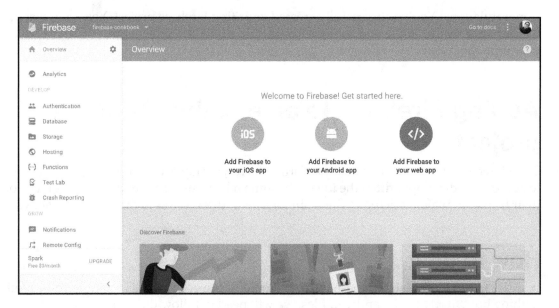

Figure 6: Firebase Application Overview/Management section.

3. Now, simply click on the magenta-colored button--**Add Firebase to your web app**--and a new model will appear holding all the required metadata (*Figure 7*):

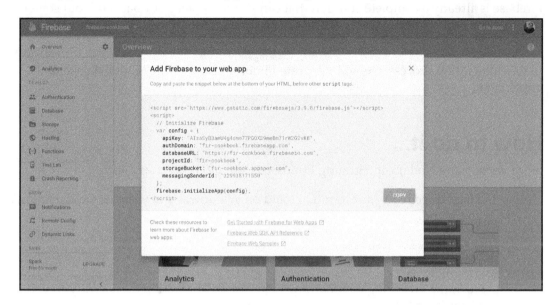

Figure 7: Firebase project credentials

4. Now simply copy and paste the code snippet on the screen into your index.html **page and you're good to go.**

Congratulations, you've successfully integrated Firebase within your Firebase project. Do keep in mind that Firebase services are very modular, so you won't have that heavyweight large dependency that you could simply exploit one--or at most four--resources from.

For the next module, we will see how we can integrate Firebase with our backend application.

How it works...

In the previous steps, we integrated the Firebase JavaScript client over our web page, and we also created the basic backbone configuration. Following the documentation guidelines, we copied/pasted the configuration script that would hold all the required tokens and API keys that Firebase was going to need in order to support our functionalities.

Integrating Firebase into the backend

Firebase is already a complete solution that can simply replace our backend, but sometimes, due to some requirements, you will find yourself integrating Firebase into the already present backend.

In this integration process, we will integrate Firebase services in a NodeJS backend application.

How to do it...

Since we're using NodeJS, integrating Firebase is one module setup away:

1. Head directly to your terminal (cmd on Windows) and write down the following command:

```
~ cd project-directory
~/project-directory ~> npm install firebase --save
```

Now, the preceding command will go and download Firebase locally so you can access it directly using your normal commonJS workflow.

2. Now, you will need to grab yourself a copy of your Firebase project configuration. This step is relatively easy as you can find the required configuration metadata by following the steps mentioned in the previous section, *Adding Firebase to an existing frontend project*, where we introduced how we can add Firebase to a frontend project.

3. Head directly to your favorite code editor and write down the following:

```
// [*] 1: requiring/importing Firebase in our
   workflow
   const firebase =  require('firebase');

// [*] 2:Initialising our application with our
   credentials
     var config = {
     apiKey: "<API_KEY>",
     authDomain: "<PROJECT_ID>.firebaseapp.com",
     databaseURL:
       "https://<DATABASE_NAME>.firebaseio.com",
     storageBucket: "<BUCKET>.appspot.com",
   };
   firebase.initializeApp(config);
```

Congratulations, you've successfully integrated Firebase within your backend workflow. I also want to point out that we can extend the workflow we have now using something called Firebase Admin SDK. We will cover how we integrate it and work with it in Chapter 7, *Firebase Admin SDK*.

How it works...

Similar to the frontend integration, in our backend we are doing the following:

1. Using a node package manager or npm to install the Firebase commonJS library, where we will find all the necessary APIs.
2. We're requiring/importing Firebase to be part our application, passing it to the configuration object that will hold all our API keys, links, and more.
3. Lastly, we're initializing our application with the configuration object we just created.

Integrating Firebase in Android applications

With Android Studio 2.0 and up, the Android Studio IDE becomes more Firebase friendly and the process of integrating Firebase's different components is nothing but a pleasing experience.

Getting ready

In order to create a Firebase Android-ready application, you need to make sure that Android Studio is present on your development machine. You can download the suitable version that suits your development machine operating system at https://developer. android.com/studio/index.html.

How to do it...

After successfully downloading the Android Studio, launch it and you will be greeted with the following screen (*Figure 8*):

Figure 8: Android Studio welcome screen

Now, let's create a new application. The process is straightforward, and is as follows:

1. When you fill in the application name, application type, and suitable used SDK, your Android application development workflow will look something like this (*Figure 9*):

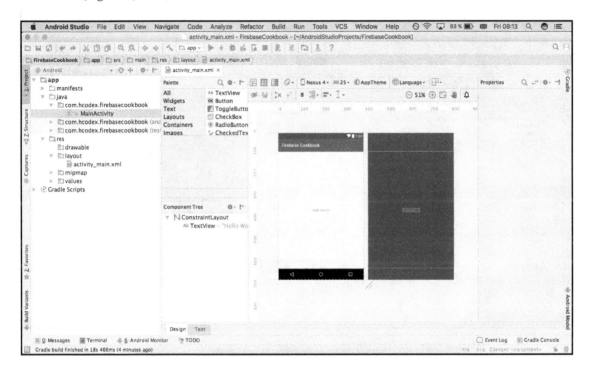

Figure 9: Android Studio after application launch

2. Now the fun can begin. Head directly to the Android Studio menu bar. Click on the **Tools** menu option and you will see a menu item that includes many options including **Firebase** (*Figure 10*):

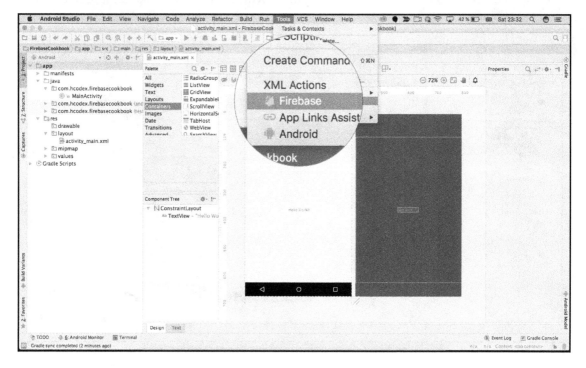

Figure 10: Integrating Firebase in our Android application

3. After clicking on it, go to the right side, to the **Assistant** section. There you will find the Firebase section, with all the goods that it can offer (*Figure 11*):

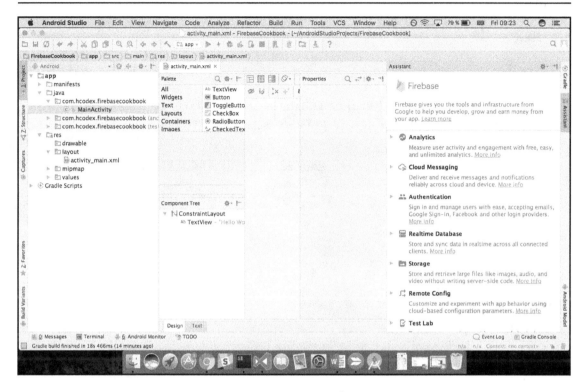

Figure 11: Android Firebase integration - part one

In this section, you will see all that Firebase has to offer--there are different sections and areas as we talked about previously. Firebase is a set of services, which means that each part is a service in itself. This also means that you're free to select whatever service you want to include. For the sake of this chapter, we're taking the Realtime Database as the option to finalize the integration process.

The integration process used in this example is applicable to all sorts of Firebase services in the exact same way.

4. After clicking on the **Realtime Database** option you will get a submenu with a simple explanation or description as to what the service actually does (*Figure 12*):

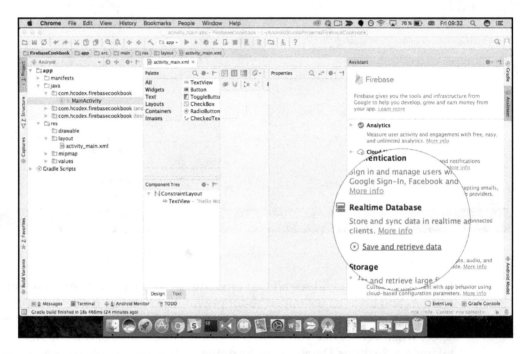

Figure 12: Android Firebase integration - part two

5. Now, simply click on the **Save and retrieve data** link option and you will start a new process that will combine both authenticating as well as download and install the Firebase component in your application (*Figure 13*):

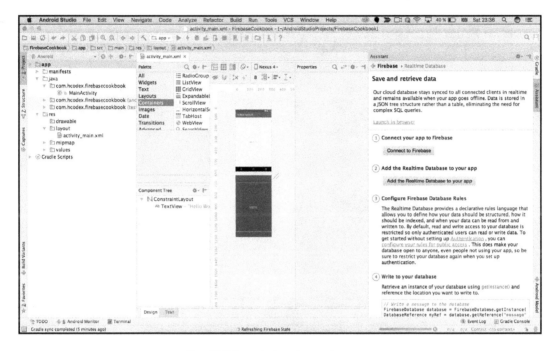

Figure 13: Firebase project integration - part three

You will need to configure your project by following the previous instructions. Next, you will need to authenticate and use the Gmail account related to your Firebase project.

6. Once you have clicked on the link, you will need to select the Google account linked to your project. In doing so, you will need to authorize Android Studio to use your Google account. Then, whenever you approve those authorization rules, you will be redirected to the following page (*Figure 14*):

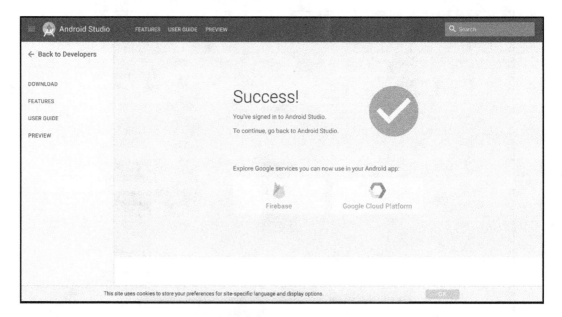

Figure 14: Firebase project integration - part four

Congratulations! Android Studio is now fully connected to your Google account. By now, you will see a new model popping up in your Android Studio. As mentioned previously, you will need to either select or create a new Firebase project. In our case, we have already created our awesome project, so we will only need to select it and hit the **Connect to Firebase** button (*Figure 15*).

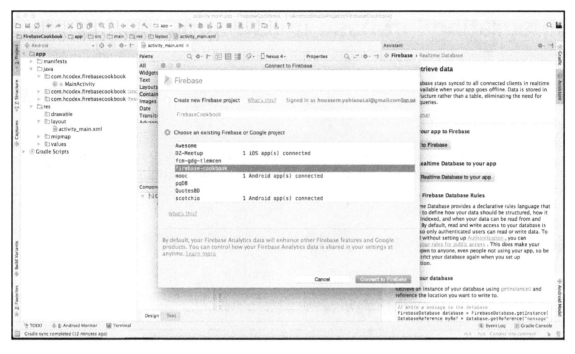

Figure 15: Firebase project integration - part five

Now, Android Studio will take some seconds to connect to your project and configure your awesome application. Then you will get the following lovely green button from heaven, indicating that everything went smoothly (*Figure 16*).

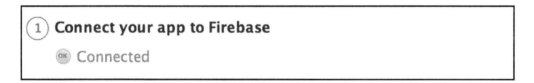

Figure 16: Firebase project integration - part six

Congratulations! Your application is now fully connected and well prepared to host your Firebase logic; all you need to do next is to integrate the service you want the most and simply work with it. We will see all that and more starting from `Chapter 11`, *Integrating Firebase with Android/iOS Natively*.

Integrating Firebase in iOS applications

Integrating Firebase our iOS application involves adding the Firebase package similar to any other package you have probably worked with in the past.

Getting ready

In order to create and integrate Firebase within your application, you will need to have a MacBook Pro or one of Apple's computer variants so that you can follow the upcoming steps; you will also need to install Xcode.

How to do it...

In order to create an iOS application, open Xcode and follow the given steps:

1. Create a new project or open your already created project (*Figure 17*):

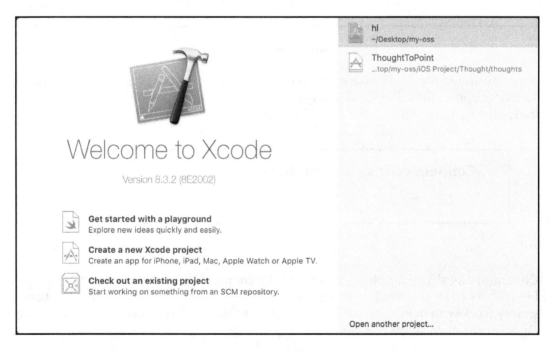

Figure 17: Xcode project opening/creation

2. In our case, we're about to start a new project called `firebasecookbook`. It's going to be based on the Xcode single-view application project template.

 In our application--or when it comes to an example provided in this book regarding Firebase and iOS--we will work with Swift instead. It's just a personal preference, but you can use the one that suits you best.

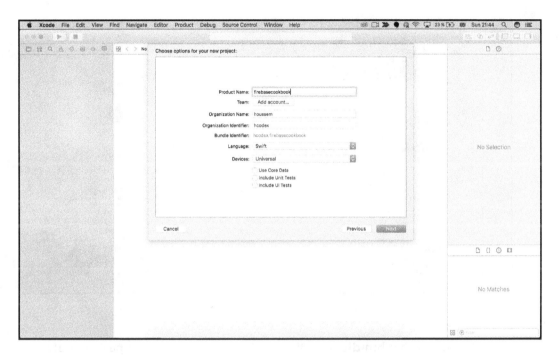

Figure 18: Xcode project creation

Don't forget to copy that **Bundle Identifier**, because we will need it in the next step. In this case, our **Bundle Identifier** is `hcodex.firebasecookbook`.

3. Go to your Firebase dashboard and click on the **Add Firebase to your iOS app** button. After clicking on it, you will get a configuration model with some steps that will guide you in your Firebase iOS integration (*Figure 19*).

Figure 19: Xcode project creation

4. Remember that **bundle id** or **Bundle Identifier**? Copy and paste that ID in its designated place and add a nickname for your application if you wish. Click on the **REGISTER APP** button.

5. Next, we will need to download a special `plist` file called the `GoogleService-info.plist` file. This file will have all the necessary metadata that will be included in your project (*Figure 20*).

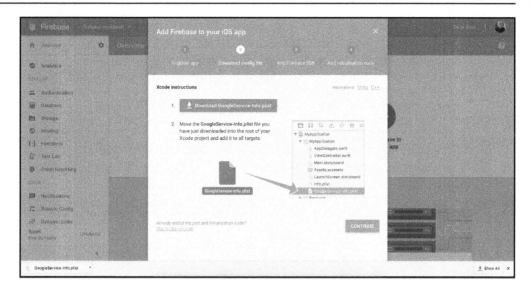

Figure 20: Firebase GoogleService-info.plist download

6. Now simply copy and paste that file into your project (*Figure 21*):

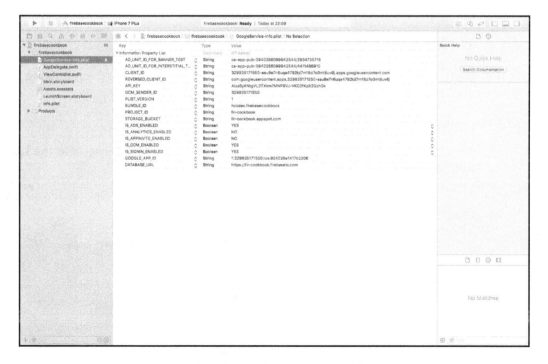

Figure 21: Firebase GoogleService-info.plist in our application.

7. After we have finished the file download and file integration, let's just install some dependencies. In this process, we will use CocoaPods as our package manager. Head directly to your project using your terminal:

```
~ cd project-directory
~/project-directory ~> pod init
```

 To download and install CocoaPods on your macOS development machine, please follow the steps mentioned on the official website: https://guides.cocoapods.org/using/getting-started.html.

After you initialize your project with CocoaPods, you will find a newly created file named `Podfile`.

 The `Podfile` is a specification that describes the dependencies of the targets of one or more Xcode projects.

8. Now, you will need to edit the `Podfile` using your favorite code or text editor and add the following line:

```
pod 'Firebase/Core'
```

9. Now, save the file, go back to your terminal, and write down the following command:

```
~/project-directory ~> pod install
```

This command will download and install all the required libraries and modules that Firebase needs to fire up within your application.

10. Now, instead of your regular project, open another special project extension, as the following command shows:

```
~/project-directory ~> open project-name.xcworkspace
```

11. We're one step behind. Now, in your application, go directly to your `AppDelegate` and simply import Firebase using the following code snippet:

```
import Firebase
```

12. Now, in the `didFinishLaunchingWithOptions` method, add the following code:

```
FIRApp.configure()
```

Congratulations! You've successfully integrated Firebase with your iOS application.

2

Firebase Real-Time Database

In this chapter, we'll cover the following topics:

- Saving and serving data in and from our Realtime Database
- Updating and deleting data from our Realtime Database
- Structuring data within our Realtime Database
- Implementing offline capabilities support

Introduction

The Firebase Realtime Database is a developer's most used product within the whole stack of the products available with Firebase. It offers dynamic, extensible functions, and almost all Realtime data insertions, updation, and deletion.

What makes Firebase Realtime Database an attractive feature among other Firebase products in the stack is its built-in broadcast functionality and an extremely simple to use API. These APIs provide the developers with an opportunity to exploit the APIs on a greater scale no matter which ecosystem and environment they are using. Besides, the Firebase Realtime Database comes with offline support. This feature simply kicks in when the app is in a not-so-reliable network state. Within this chapter, we're going through its different usages and will talk about the different use cases that will add more real-time look and feel to your application along with offline support without adding any third party utility.

Saving and serving data in and from our Realtime Database

When thinking of web apps, the saving/serving data process is essential. Data is typically the backbone of any web application, and saving is what most tutorials or guides describe as persisting it into a database.

Firebase is not exactly a database but is very similar to other databases that you might find on the market these days. It's a NoSQL database with Realtime functionality built into it, which means that when you save (persist) data into it, it will automatically broadcast the channels to anyone who is listening, typically all your users, also known as consumers.

In this chapter, we'll see how we can exploit the awesome Firebase Realtime Database to save/serve our data.

How to do it...

1. We will first talk about the initial part of the recipe, which involves saving data in Firebase. So, let's see how that's done. Before we start with how we can save our data within our database, let's take a look at our application and the way it looks. Head to your Firebase project dashboard's Database section, and you will find something that looks pretty much like this (*Figure 1*):

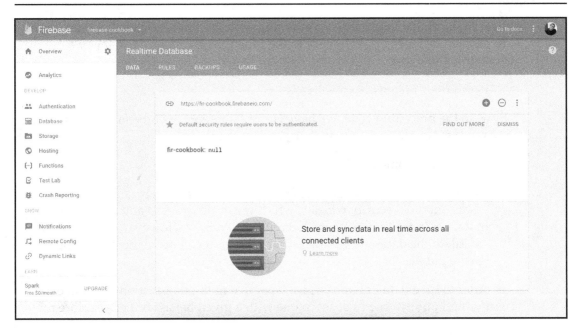

Figure 1: Showcasing the Blank Firebase Realtime Database.

2. If you have any experience with web development or data nature, you will recognize that our data will be saved in JSON format. This is actually quite good, as it will mean less time processing and searching for data, so NoSQL idle that we usually have to deal with a relational SQL-based database.

3. If you remember the Integration step in `Chapter 1`, *Firebase - Getting Started*, there's a special link called `databaseURL` that is essential for us now because we want to add more data to our database.

4. Bear in mind that in order to do anything with the Firebase client, you will need to have an instance or a reference to the functionality required so that we can do something like this:

```
var db = firebase.database();
```

Now, in the preceding code, we have created a reference of the Firebase database reference for ourselves. Now we can work using it.

Now, let's write some data!

By default, the data read/write functionalities, are used by authenticated users only for security reasons, which means in order to add or get any data, you need to be authenticated using Firebase. However, with a simple tweak to the database authorization rules, you can make the process open to the public.

5. In order to save data in Firebase, we have two methods/functions; we have the set() and push() methods, each one with a given behavior. Let's explore them:

```
db.ref('packtpub/' +1234).set({
    name: "Houssem Yahiaoui",
    current_book: "Firebase Cookbook"
});
```

6. Let's see what we just did; we used the database reference that we created and simply navigated to the packtpub route to user 1234, where we introduced new data to the normal being an author.

Bear in mind that the set() method has a double effect; it will either insert the new data into path if no data has ever been introduced, or it will replace it.

7. We can see this in our database (*Figure 2*):

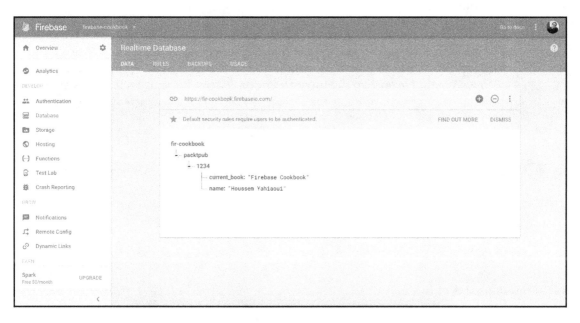

Figure 2: Firebase Realtime Database after adding some Data.

8. Moreover, we can add lists of data, for instance, when you're over a chat application, or any data that typically requires direct and autosaving with no replacing. Here, every time you push, a new node or object is being added to the database; the `push()` method gives you the ultimate solution. Also, this data will be identifiable with a unique key that is time-based:

```
db.ref('packtpub/chat').push({
    name: "Houssem Yahiaoui",
    message: "Hello All !",
    photo_url : "<link to my picture>"
});
```

We will now move on to the second part of the recipe, which teaches us about serving and reading data from Firebase:

1. In order to serve data over any Firebase application, we typically have two scenarios that we pass through, the first one is when you load our application, you typically want to grab all the data from there directly and bind it to your UI, also we want to grab also the most recent data from there as well, this is also possible using Firebase Realtime Database API, so let's see how we can implement the two scenarios.

2. So, let's suppose we have that part of our system where we just want it to read the data once, which means we don't want it to be updated with each change to the database. The Firebase API has the `once()` method, which is pretty explicit when it comes to functionality. So let's see how we can make that happen:

```
firebase.database().ref('/admins).once('value').then((snapshot)
    => {
  var admins = snapshot.val();
});
```

Let's digest what we just did:

*   We started by taking a reference to the `admins` section of our database
*   We used `once()` to grab the data that will be used just once, which means no further update of the `admins` section will raise an event
*   We're returning a `snapshot` of this final that will have the data within

3. Now, let's suppose that our data is being expected to change over time; this means that we need to keep a constant eye on it. Such a thing is really easy to implement over Firebase, using nothing but the Firebase database API. So let's see how we can make it happen:

```
var adminRef = firebase.database().ref('/admins');
adminRef.on('value',(snapshot) => {
  //implement you logic here.
});
```

How it works...

Let's explain what just happened:

1. We need to get a reference to the data we need to listen on.
2. We listen to any data changes that will go to be an event; we all know that to listen to an event, you use the `on()` function with the event name. In this case, it's the `value` event, then we find the suitable possible way to include the fresh data with the already present one.

Updating and deleting data from our Realtime Database

The update/delete functionalities are widely present in all the applications. It's simply our way to alter the data or remove it for good. So let's see how we can incorporate such functionalities over our application.

How to do it...

We will take a look at updating data first.

Updating data over Firebase was always a point of debate and discussion over StackOverflow; so for that, let's just explain the two principles over the new APIs and see how they differ from each other:

1. The `update()` function will give us the option to send simultaneous update calls to our database, and won't do anything besides the expected behavior of an update function, that is, updating the data without altering the reference of the record.
2. The `set()` function, within its behavior, changes the reference to the data itself while replacing it with a new one.
3. What matters the most for us is the behavior we seek, so the `Update` function is the most suitable function call to go with while implementing your CRUD application. Let's see how we can implement it, while thinking of one of the most requested twitter functionalities, speaking about updating tweets, of course:

```
//TODO : Define Tweet Structure.
let tweet = {};
```

```
// Get a key for a new Entry
let newTweetKey =
firebase.database().ref().child('tweets').push().key;
let uid = firebase.auth().currentUser.uid;
var</span> updates = {};
updates['/tweets/' + newTweetKey] = tweet;
updates[</span>'/user-tweets/' + uid + '/' + newTweetKey] =
  tweet;
firebase.database().ref().update(updates);
```

How it works...

So, let's talk about what just happened. Besides the fact that we revolutionized twitter, we did the following:

1. We defined the structure of our tweet.
2. We grabbed the new tweet key.
3. We grabbed the connected user uid.
4. We created a new updated object and both added a route to our overall tweets and updated the one with its given key, also the tweets will be added or saved over user's own personal tweets because we've updated both places in the same time.
5. We called the `update()` function over the root reference of our database and since we're using the schema, the Updates object will simultaneously update both fields with the needed data.

Congratulations! You've successfully updated both fields with one call. Keep in mind that the usage of `set()` will create a new entry, the thing that really doesn't want to happen while updating our data.

Let's now move on to see how to remove data from Realtime Database:

1. In order to delete data over Firebase, we simply use the `remove()` function over our data reference or simply use the `set()` function, or even the `update()` function in case we wanted to update data simultaneously, setting data to null. Let's see how we can make it happen:

```
let tweetRef = //TODO : Get Tweet Ref.
firebase.database().ref(`path/${tweetRef}`).remove();
//Or
let uid = firebase.auth().currentUser.uid;
var updates = {};
```

```
updates['/tweets/' + tweetRef] = null;
updates['/user-tweets/' + uid + '/' + tweetRef] =
 null;
firebase.database().ref().update(updates);
```

Congratulations! You just deleted a tweet! It's quite obvious now; we can use tricks within
our Firebase application that simply works outside of the box or tricks that use other
functionalities such as update() for simultaneous delete.

Structuring data within our Realtime Database

The hype over Firebase database structure is real; people just don't know how to do it. The
idea behind it is simple and clear--stop thinking in the relational world data structuring
because such thing won't simply work in a document-based architecture.

How to do it...

Firebase database is built to be dynamic and flat, so the idea of data redundancy is
somehow a must. The idea from all this is to fetch data as fast as possible, and true, in order
to add or delete data, you will need it mentioned pretty much everywhere. But that's a cost
we will pay if we want to optimize the downloading and data fetching time.

1. Let me present an example that demonstrates this thought:

```
{
  "events": {
    "firebase_summit": {
      "title": "Firebase Summit event",
      "timestamp": 1508883321
    },
    "google_io": { ... },
    "...": { ... }
  },

  "members": {
    "firebase_summit": {
      "superman": true,
      "eagleye": true,
      "charlesmountain": true
    },
    "google_io": { ... },
```

```
      "...": { ... }
    },

    "conversations": {
      "firebase_summit": {
        "c1": {
          "name": "superman",
    "message": "Please prevent any Kryptonite based
        materials
            at entrance"</span>,
          "timestamp": 1508883539
        },
        "c2": { ... },
        "c3": { ... }
      },
      "google_io": { ... },
      "...": { ... }
    },
    "users" : {
      "superman" : {
        "fullName": "Clark Kent",
        "events" : {
          "firebase_sumit" : true,
          "..."
        }
      }
    }
  }
}
```

So technically, if you note, we're adding data pretty much everywhere. This is essential for us so that we can keep fetching data; this way, retrieving it will be really fast and will save us download time.

The idea will be separate from different parts of the data, which means we will only download and retrieve all the data we want at a given time. Also, this pattern will make the security part of it easy, since we won't have any fears of users accessing data that they're not authorized to access; plus, if we saved data over a long JSON tree, knowing that it's possible, it will make us vulnerable because it will just make the security part more difficult. In addition, the wait time and extensibility of such data in the future is an impossible mission to achieve.

 The Data structure schemes was improved within another Firebase product called the Firebase Cloud FireStore, find more on that matter covered in the Appendix.

Implementing offline capabilities support

Firebase offers the offline experience outside of the box. There's no need to do any magical trick or write any piece of code; all you need to do is to focus on your application logic and exploit the Firebase API in the best way you can. All the changes you will do to the database will be synchronized once connected to a stable connectivity source.

In this recipe, we'll see how we can know whether we're simply connected to our database or not; this feature is simple but can help us enormously in improving our user experience.

Getting ready

In order to have the needed reference point within our application to support the added functionality, simply ensure that your project is fully integrated with Firebase; check Chapter 1, *Firebase - Getting Started*, for extra information.

How to do it...

1. Let's see how we can use the Firebase database API to perform the connection checking functionality:

```
let miConnected = firebase.database().ref(".info/connected");
miConnected.on("value", function(res) {
    if (res.val() === true) {
     //TODO : show connection status as connected
    } else {
     //TODO : show connection status as disconected
    }
});
```

The preceding code will simply test the connection to the server, and it depends on the value we're getting from the server; we handle the UI accordingly.

How it works...

We're just listening on a special path to determine the status of our connection to Firebase, is the value is true, means that we're fully authenticated, else, means that we're not authentication due to a network latency or no network at all.

3
File Management with Firebase Storage

In this chapter, we will cover the following recipes:

- Creating file storage references
- Implementing file upload
- Implementing file serving and downloading
- Implementing file deletion
- Implementing file metadata updates
- Firebase file storage error handling

Introduction

Just like any good build application, uploading files and saving/serving them is a traditional, well-established workflow where you typically have different methods to save your files. So in this chapter, we're going to see how we can implement one of the coolest added functionalities and talk about file storage.

File storage in Firebase lets you upload, download, and do your basic **CRUD** (**create**, **read**, **update**, and **delete**) functionalities using really simple and straightforward APIs. Also, Firebase file storage is robust, secure, and scalable like the rest of the Firebase service suite.

Creating file storage references

As you can see, everything we do in Firebase starts with creating a reference. That way, we can have a well managed and separated workflow across the different parts of our apps.

Getting ready

Before getting started with the code we need to confirm the presence of the following configuration:

1. That you have a Firebase project, and you've properly configured it, if this is not the case, please check Chapter 1, *Firebase - Getting Started*, for that.
2. you need to make sure that the "**storageBucket**" field is present with its bucket link, this one will be the place where all your files will live underneath.

How to do it...

If you followed the steps in Chapter 1, *Firebase - Getting Started*, you will have an idea of how we can integrate Firebase into our workflow.

1. We're going to assume that we're in a web workflow. So this recipe will demonstrate the basic steps of having references in Firebase Storage using the following code snippet:

```
//Creating a reference that point to the root
  directory.
let packtRef = firebase.storage().ref();
```

What we've done here is simply created a reference to the root directory; it's basically your application root directory where all your files and other folders will affiliate from.

2. Now let's see how we can get a reference for a created folder or even files in Firebase Storage using the following code block:

```
//Creating a reference for the books directory.
  let packtBooks = packtRef.child('books');
//Creating a reference for the Firebase Cookbook
   file.
  let firebaseCookbook =
  packtBooks.child('Fiebase_Cookbook.ebook');
```

How it works...

Within our root directory, we have another subfolder named `books`. It will typically be a child in the root directory. This is why, just like the files, the structure looks like that of a database--a *tree* where we have a *root*, *branches* or *children*, and *leaves* acting as our end files. Let us now see what we did in the recipe:

- Now, you might wonder: how can I get the final path or even the name of a file or a directory? The APIs to do this are quite explicit, as shown in the following code:

```
//Getting the file Path.
let bookPath = firebaseCookbook.fullPath;

//Getting the file Name.
let bookName = firebaseCookbook.name;
```

So what just happened again? Basically, we got the file path, which is `books/Firebase_Cookbook.ebook`. What about the name of the file? Well, you guessed it right, it's `Firebase_Cookbook.ebook`.

In `Chapter 4`, *Firebase Authentication*, we're going to see how we can implement the file upload mechanism within our application.

Implementing file upload

We're going to cover how we can we implement file upload in our application following a really cool example we're going to build

The example contains one single application with a button that will open the file picker. Once the file is selected the **Upload** process will start, so let's see how we can make this process happen.

How to do it...

1. To upload a file, we need to first create a new reference to the created file. We already know that we got a reference to the root folder, as we saw it earlier in this chapter. The code for creating a new reference to the created file is as follows:

```
//Creating a new reference for the uploaded file.
let imageRef = packtRef.child(`images/${<imageName>.
 <ext>}`);
```

2. You may wonder how can we programmatically create a folder. The current API doesn't have that capability, but Firebase does it automatically. This means that since we know we're pointing to a file that is in the `images` folder or any sub-folder, Firebase will go and create that folder for us dynamically.

 Don't forget to add the filename and it's extension once you create a new file reference. By this, I mean that you need to provide the full wanted path for the file otherwise you will face some unexpected behavior from the Firebase console.

3. Now, to get the actual file, we typically have two ways--we use the files or the blob APIs and then we push the file directly to the Firebase API using the `put()` method. The following example explains the use of the Firebase file upload using a normal, good file input.

I've created a simple page with a simple upload input and some basic awesome logic behind it. The following screenshot shows that page:

Figure 1: End result of the application we're building.

4. Now let's look at and digest the code behind this page. Implement the following code for creating your own page:

```html
<body class="container">
  <div class="text-center">
    <img src="img/firebase.png">
  </div>
  <div class="row text-center">
    <div class="image-upload">
      <label for="file-input">
        <span class="attach-doc">Upload to
         Firebase  <i
        class="fa fa-upload" aria-hidden="true">
         </i></span>
      </label>
      <input id="file-input" type="file"
      onchange="uploadToFirebase(this.files)"/>
    </div>
  </div>
</div>
```

5. The preceding code represents the HTML structure of our minimal web page. Next, let's look at the custom behavior that manages the page in the following code snippet:

```html
<script src="https://www.gstatic.com/firebasejs/4.1.1/
firebase.js">
 </script>
  <script>
   var config = {/*Your Firebase config object, found
  over the Firebase console, see how to get it over
     chapter 1*/}
   //Getting a reference for our input file.
  let upload = document.getElementById('file-input');
    upload.addEventListener('change',
      uploadToFirebase, false);
   //Let's implement the onchange function.
   function uploadToFirebase(files) {
  //Getting the root ref from the Firebase Storage.
    let rootRef = firebase.storage().ref();
    let file = files[0]; //Getting the file from
     the Files Apis.
    let fileRef =
    rootRef.child(`images/${file.name}`);
    fileRef.put(file)
      .then(() => {
       console.log('your images was uploaded !');
```

```
            })
            .catch(err => console.log(err));
        }
    </script>
```

6. After clicking on the **Upload to Firebase** button, we're going to see the following error in our **Chrome Dev Tools Console** (*Figure 2*):

Figure 2: Error generated from Firebase because of authorization

Now, this error is coming from the authorization rules in our Firebase console. This indicates that we did not dispose the right privileges in order to upload our file to Firebase's **Storage** bucket.

7. To fix this issue, head directly to the rules section in the Firebase **Storage** bucket (*Figure 3*):

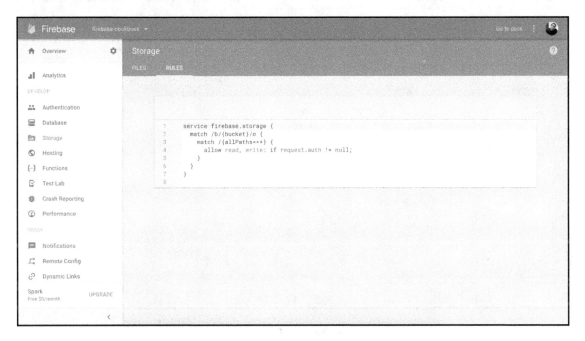

Figure 3: Default Authorization rules for any Firebase project

8. Change line 4 from its current state to the following (*Figure 4*):

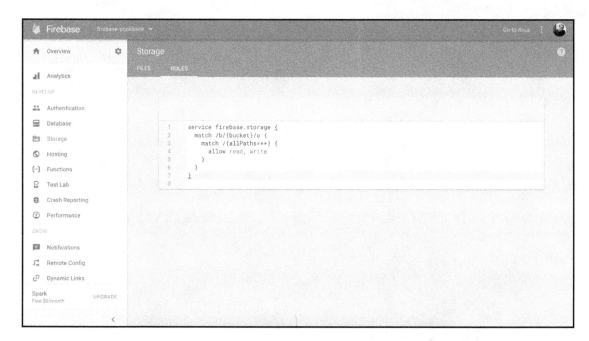

Figure 4: After changing the current Authorization rules

So, typically we're allowing `read` and `write` for all paths, without any authentication or authorization checks.

9. By now, we only need to refresh the page and upload our file in the normal way. Once that is done, we will have the following in the Firebase **Storage** bucket (*Figure 5*):

Figure 5: Showcasing of the created folder

Inside our images folder, we will find the uploaded image.

How it works...

Let's explain how it works:

1. We created a minimal web page with an upload input, that had an event listener for the change event.

2. When we clicked on the **Upload to Firebase** button, which is a nice-looking input button, we selected a file then grabbed it using the file APIs (built into the browser itself).

3. We created and grabbed ourselves a reference to the root directory and for the file, we wanted to upload.

4. We used a special Firebase method called put(), which returns a promise. That promise was resolved when we successfully uploaded the file.

5. We maintained the authorization rules for our file upload, keeping in mind that this was implemented for development. In a production-ready environment, maintaining the right rules would be highly essential.

Implementing file serving and downloading

In the previous recipe, we discussed how we could upload files to the **Storage** bucket. In this part of the chapter, we're going to see how we can deliver and download our files directly from the **Storage** bucket.

How to do it...

Typically, we don't have a way to showcase all the files we have within our bucket. We do have files and folders in Firebase; however there's no API to showcase folders, but only to showcase files.

 Bear in mind that the notion of folders doesn't have a meaning within the platform. This means that there's nothing called a folder within the API or logic--it's just a basic path reference to our files.

Thus, we need to have our own custom logic for the folder showcasing, typically a local database where you can save your basic files metadata. However, that is out of the scope of this chapter.

1. As we did previously, we need to create ourselves a reference for the required file:

```
//Getting the file reference.
var rootRef = firebase.storage().ref();
var imageRef = rootRef.child('images/<image-name>.
  <image-ext>');
```

2. Next, let's use the `getDownloadURL()` function so that we can get our download URL:

```
imageRef.getDownloadURL()
  .then((url) => {
      //Getting the download URL.
      console.log(url);
  })
  .catch(err => console.log(err));
```

3. When the `getDownloadURL()` function is resolved, we will have the file download URL, and we can use it for our needs, as shown follows (*Figure 6*):

```
Download Url : https://firebasestorage.googleapis.com/v0/b/fir-cookbook.appspot.com/o/imag…t%2011.44.18%20AM.p   index.html:71
ng?alt=media&token=e39d5a92-811c-4227-bb26-ba6cb9536a68
file uploaded with success congrats                                                                             index.html:65
>
```

Figure 6: File download link

Congratulations! By now, we have the downloadable URL with us. We can use this for our needs later on, even by saving it to a local database, which is preferable.

How it works...

In the preceding code, we did the following :

1. Grabbed a reference for our file. (Don't forget to have an active reference, a file selection, or something similar so you can have the active reference.)
2. After getting the reference, we called for the API to get the download URL. This can be exploited over the image source in case the file was an image. You can even use `fetch` to download it locally, so the possibilities are endless here.

Implementing file deletion

Up until now, we have managed to upload and download our files from the **Storage** bucket, but sometimes we really want to delete the files we uploaded previously. This is doable using the Firebase Storage bucket APIs we used in the previous two sections.

How to do it...

1. As we discussed in the previous chapters before we do anything we need to grab ourselves a reference for the wanted file, so let's do that! The code for creating a reference is given as follows:

```
//Getting the Root Folder Reference.
var rootRef = firebase.storage().ref();
var imageRef = rootRef.child('images/<image-name>.
  <image-ext>');
```

2. Now let's use a special method or function that will help us to delete this particular file. We're talking about the delete() method, which we will see how to implement using the following code:

```
imageRef.delete()
  .then(() => {
  //We successfully deleted the file.
  })
  .catch(err => {
  //Report/Showcase the error.
  });
```

 Again, the filename and its extension need to be grabbed from a custom logic of your own. That is done by using a local database that holds a small metadata fingerprint of the file after you upload it. Later on, whenever you want to do any kind of custom logic, it will be with ease.

Congratulations! By now, you have successfully learned how to delete the file that you do not want. In the next recipe, we're going to see how we can update the file metadata.

Implementing file metadata updates

So typically, any kind of file--or folder for that matter--has what we call metadata. That vital information is present to help recognize the nature of the file and its type. It's what we normally refer to for adding MIME types, and files in the Firebase Storage bucket are no exception. Within the platform, the possibilities present are let us retrieve and also update the file's metadata, and in this recipe, we're going to see how we can do just that.

How to do it...

1. Let's start first with retrieving metadata. To allow us to do so, the Firebase APIs provide us with a function called `getMetadata()`. This function will allow for the retrieving of all file metadata in one place, but first, let's grab a file reference as we did in the earlier recipes:

```
//Grab a reference for the Root Directory.
let rootRef = firebase.storage().ref();

//Let's grab a reference for our file.
let imageRef = rootRef.child('path-to-file/<file-
 name>.<file-ext>');

//No let's get the file metadata.
imageRef.getMetadata()
     .then((meta) => {
//Meta function parameter represent our file metadata.
        console.log(meta);
     })
  .catch(err => console.log(err));
```

   Congratulations, by now you've successfully got the metadata of the file that you wanted. It's up to you to decide the showcasing method, as now you can display them.

2. As a final step, you might wonder about errors. Is there anything special about them? Is there any way to properly showcase custom error messages with different kinds of errors?

   All these questions are legit, and for bonus points, we're going to see how we can digest Firebase error handling in the next recipe.

Firebase file storage error handling

If you're serious about your next big product or application, you will instantly recognize that the proper showcasing of error on the client side is a serious and urgent matter. In this recipe, I will demonstrate how you can get and read Firebase Storage errors properly.

If you recognized the pattern we used throughout the recipes, you will probably find out--even if you're not familiar with JavaScript's promises--that we're getting all our error message from Firebase in the catchphrase.

JavaScript promise APIs are relatively new APIs shipped in the ES2015. You can read more about them, and how you can implement them within your own code, here: `https://developer.mozilla.org/en/docs/Web/JavaScript/Reference/Global_Objects/Promise`.

How to do it...

1. Let's look at an example. Suppose we're deleting a file; let's now see how we can formulate our error messages based on the error type:

```
//Deleting an image from the bucket.
 imageRef.getMetadata()
   .then((meta) => {
//Meta function parameter represent our file metadata.
        console.log(meta);
     })
     .catch(err => {
          switch (err.code) {
               case 'storage/unknown':
               break;
               case 'storage/object_not_found':
               breaks;
               case : 'storage/project_not_found':
               breaks;
               case : 'storage/unauthenticated':
               breaks;
               case : 'storage/unauthorized':
               breaks;
               ..
               ...
               ....
          }
     });
```

2. Switching over the `err.code` type, we'll get a string that represents the error type we're facing. Then we can provide the proper showcasing of the error, with the help of which we can have a UX ready application. This happens because providing the explicit error message can save time on the user side, as well as money for us as the application creators.

 In the preceding code block, we covered a small set of error messages that we might have. You can read more in the official documentation, and incorporate the error message that you think suits your application the most: `https://firebase.google.com/docs/storage/web/handle-errors`.

This wraps up everything we have done with Firebase Storage bucket APIs. Now you can build and incorporate the service with confidence in your exciting new application.

4
Firebase Authentication

In this chapter, we're going to cover the following recipes:

- Implementing email/password authentication
- Implementing anonymous authentication
- Implementing Facebook login
- Implementing Twitter login
- Implementing Google Sign-in
- Implementing user metadata retrieval
- Implementing the linking of multiple authentication providers

Introduction

If you're a web developer, you will have recognized that building a secure, well balanced, and proven authentication system is a really tedious job to do even though it's just emails and passwords.

Nowadays, web applications are using social login and it's one of the most used and requested features in today's web scene. It's an easy and quick way to authenticate and login to a web application using your daily OAuth, from Facebook to Google Plus and Twitter, even GitHub if you're building a community-based application.

> "**OAuth** or **Open Authentication** is an open protocol that allows secure authorization in a simple and standard method from web, mobile and desktop applications."
>
> - OAuth community

Firebase is here to help you with secure login by providing multi-authentication methods, for example, an email/password and social login with major providers. It even provides a way for anonymous login to happen and it is a well secured, efficient way to manage authentication in your web application. In this chapter, we're going to see how can we use it.

Implementing email/password authentication

In this recipe, we're going to demonstrate how we can implement password authentication from a really simple, widespread example scenario that is present in many different web applications. The following is a screenshot of the Firebase application supporting email/password authentication:

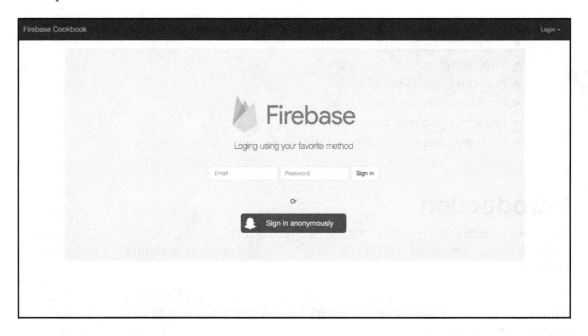

Figure 1: Basic application supporting email/password authentication

How to do it...

1. In the previous figure, we saw a simple login page with **Email** and **Password** fields and another button for anonymous login. First, let's see the code behind it:

```html
<div class="container">
  <div class="jumbotron">
    <div class="text-center">
        <img src="img/firebase.png">
<p style="margin-top:-50px">Log in using your
 favorite method</p>
    </div>
    <form class="form-inline text-center">
        <div class="form-group">
          <label class="sr-only" for="email">Email
           address</label>
          <input type="email" class="form-control"
        id="email">
        </div>
        <div class="form-group">
           <label class="sr-only"
           for="password">Password</label>
           <input type="password" class="form-
             control"
             id="password">
      </div>
      <button id="login" class="btn btn-
        default">Sign in</button>
    </form><br><br>
    <div class="text-center">Or</div><br>
    <div class="text-center">
      <a class="btn btn-social btn-lg btn-github"
        style="width:
      260px" id="anonymousLogin">
        <span class="fa fa-snapchat-ghost"></span>
        Sign in anonymously
      </a>
    </div>
  </div>
</div>
```

2. In order to make this page functional and start using the APIs, we need to toggle some buttons first in the Firebase console. Go to **Project Dashboard** | **Authentication** | SIGN-IN METHOD as shown in the following figure:

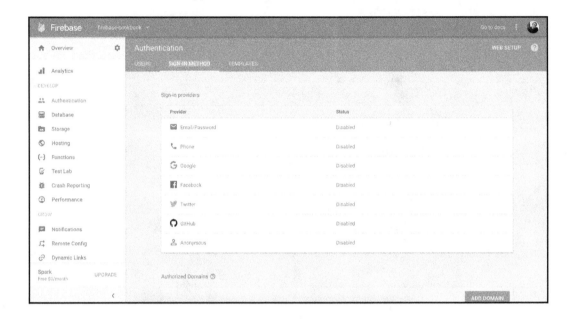

Figure 2: Firebase project console--authentication section

3. Now, you toggle the authentication methods you want. In our case, we want **Email/Password** and **Anonymous** as well. Simply click on the **Enable** switch and then click on the **SAVE** button, as shown in the following screenshot:

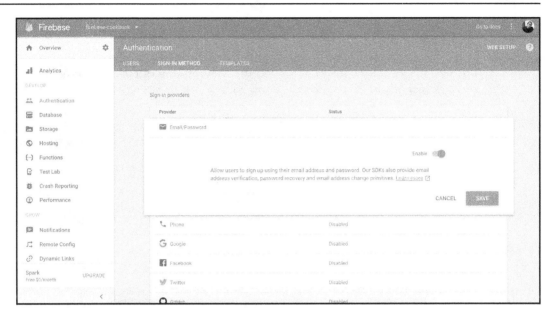

Figure 3: Activating email/password authentication from Firebase project console

4. After activating these two methods, let's see how we can use the APIs. Create a new account for a new user.

5. Once we have successfully created the new user account, let's log in to our account using the following code:

```
//Getting the Email/Password and Signin button from
the inputs above.
let email = document.getElementById('email').value;
let password =
  document.getElementById('password').value;
let signIn = document.getElementById('login');

//Listening on the signIn button click.
signIn.addEventListener('click', (ev) => {
  firebase.auth().signInWithEmailAndPassword(
      email,password)
      .then(user => {
        //Handling the successful authentication.
      })
      .catch(function(error) {
        //Handling the error showcasing.
      });
  }, false);
});
```

Now, it's up to you to to make the transition and deliver the proper UI to the user after successful login.

6. But you might think since I'm logged in, I need to log out as well. Well, that process is really easy, as the following code block demonstrates:

```
//Getting a reference for our Logout Button.
let logoutBtn = document.getElementById('logout');
logoutBtn.addEventListener('click', (ev)) {
    firebase.auth().logout()
        .then(() => {
//Redirect to the Home page or any custom login here.
        })
        .catch(err => {
//Getting the error and properly   showcasing it here.
        });
}, false);
```

Congratulations, you've successfully implemented the login/logout functionalities in your application.

Implementing anonymous authentication

You might wonder why we need this. Since it's anonymous, it means that we don't have an identity on our system. That is true, but sometimes we want to have protected content that we deliver to our authorized users. So by using this method, we allow non-users to have a temporary account to experience the app. But if they, for instance, decide to create an account, we can provide them the option of linking their sign-in account to an anonymous one.

How to do it...

1. In order to do this, we will use the Firebase auth APIs like we did previously, as shown in the following code snippet:

```
//Get a button reference.
let anonLogin =
  document.getElementById('anonymousLogin');
anonLogin.addEventListener('click', () => {
    firebase.auth().signInAnonymously()
        .catch(err => {
            //Catch and showcase the error.
```

```
            });
    }, false);
```

2. Now, we need another way to check whether the user is logged in or not. To do that we'll need to check the authentication state of the user, using the onAuthStateChanged event as shown in the following code:

```
firebase.auth().onAuthStateChanged((user) => {
    if (user) {
// Since we have the user object, we have a stable
      connection, and we're // authenticated.
      var uid = user.uid;
    } else {
      // User is signed out.
    }
});
```

What just happened?

Typically, the onAuthStateChanged event is going to be executed once the authentication state of a user changes. So it's going to be fired if the user logs in or logs out of their account. We can learn the current state of a user via the user object. If the insertion is true, we're authenticated. The else condition would mean that either the user just logged out or we're simply not connected.

Implementing Facebook login

If you have tried surfing recent web apps, you will definitely be able to recognize the famous *Sign in with Facebook*. It is a really lovely, easy, and fast way to authenticate a user nowadays. We can bring all the basic metadata such as full name, image, email address, and basic information directly from the Facebook servers.

In this recipe, we're going to see how we can implement the Facebook login functionality in our application.

Getting ready

Before starting, we'll need to create a Facebook app. To do so, please head directly to the Facebook Developer platform at `https://developers.facebook.com`. You will see a dashboard, as shown in the following screenshot:

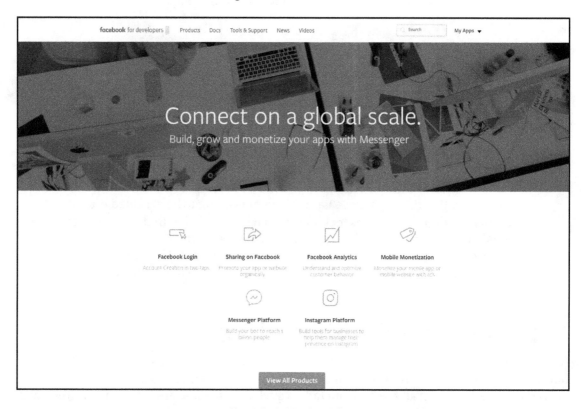

Figure 4: Facebook Developer platform

If you hover over **My Apps**, you will see a list of all your current Facebook apps. For our requirements, we'll create a new one. To do that, simply click the **Add a New App** option, as shown in the following screenshot:

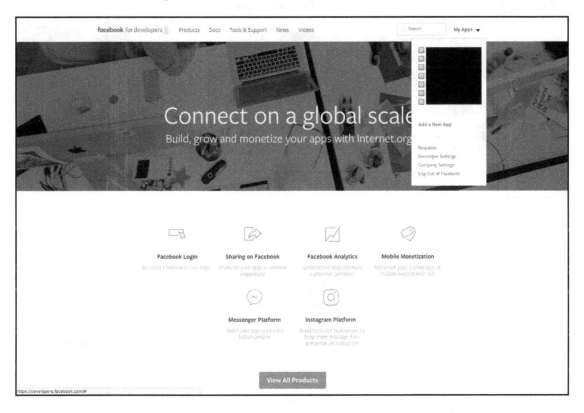

Figure 5: Adding a new Facebook application

Next, we have the following modal, where you can add your application's basic information:

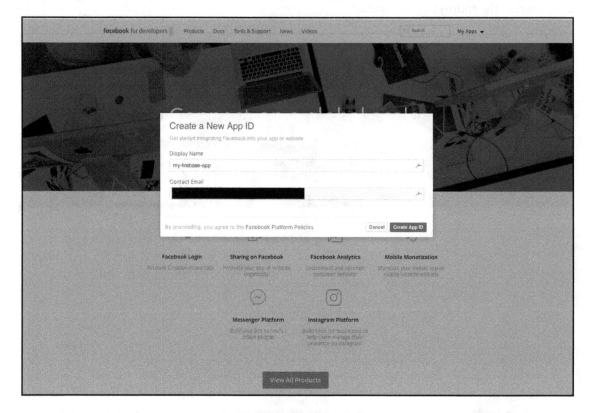

Figure 6: Giving the application's basic metadata

Click on the **Create App ID** button. Now your application will be created and you will be redirected to your application console.

As we saw previously, in order to incorporate any of the Firebase authentication methods, we need to activate them first. Go back to **Project Dashboard** | **Authentication** | **SIGN-IN METHOD**. Copy/paste your **App ID** and **App secret** from your Facebook console application to these sections in your Firebase **Authentication** section:

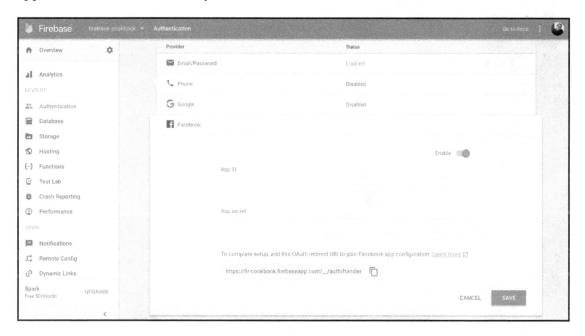

Figure 7: Activating Facebook authentication from the Firebase project console

Now, to finish the configuration, copy the link shown and paste it here:

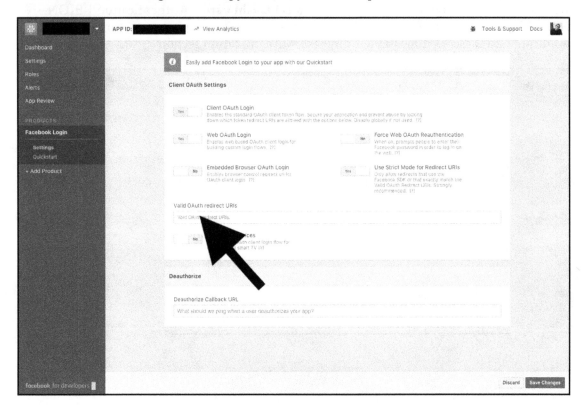

Figure 8: Adding the link from Firebase to our Facebook app

Now simply click on the **Save Changes** button, and with that, we're done.

How to do it...

1. By now, your console is well configured. Let's add some logic from the Facebook login button to the Firebase authentication API call:

Figure 9: Basic application - adding a Facebook OAuth button

2. Next, let's hook our button with an event listener and introduce the logic behind the Firebase Facebook sign-in method:

```
let facebookLogin =
document.getElementById('fcbLogin');
facebookLogin.addEventListener('click', () => {
    //TODO HERE : ADD LOGIC
}, false);
```

3. Before we call the authentication Firebase function, we need to configure the authentication provider, as the following code shows:

```
// 1. Get a FacebookAuthProvider instance.
let facebookProvider = new
firebase.auth.FacebookAuthProvider();

//2. Add some permissions and scopes (optional)
 facebookProvider.addScope('public_profile');
```

If you want to find out all the supported Facebook scopes, head to the official documentation via this link: `https://developers.facebook.com/docs/facebook-login/permissi` `onse`.

4. After setting up the necessary provider object, let's make the call to the Firebase API:

```
firebase.auth().signInWithPopup(facebookProvider)
    .then(function(result) {
        console.log(result);
        let user = result.user;
    }).catch(function(error) {
        // TODO: Handle Errors.
    });
```

5. After calling this function, let's reload the page and click the Facebook authentication button. The result will look like the following screenshot:

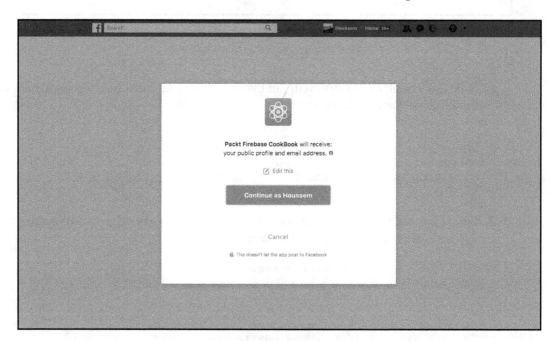

Figure 10: Using your Facebook profile to authorize the Facebook application to log in

The results are as expected--we're moving toward the Facebook application authorization page where we use our own Facebook account to proceed with the connection, which is awesome!

If you open your DevTools console, you will find the authentication results with all the information that you'd expect. You will be able to see all sorts of tokens pertaining to the `user` object containing the public profile you asked for before, which holds the display name, photo URL, and email.

As soon as you click on the Facebook authentication button, you'll be redirected to another page. It's the default behavior given that once you authorize the application, you will be redirected back to the actual application page. This behavior can be overridden using the provider object we created previously, by adding the following:

```
provider.setCustomParameters({
  'display': 'popup'
});
```

This will display the authentication page over a modal so you don't go back and forth between pages.

With that, you've successfully implemented Facebook authentication using Firebase.

Implementing Twitter login

Twitter is the most used social media platform in the world, with more than 300 million active users. We can't simply forget about incorporating it into our application. In this recipe, we're going to see how we can activate and implement Twitter authentication using the Firebase API.

Getting ready

Before we start the coding part, we need to make some configurations within our application. Head to your **Firebase Console** | **Authentication** | **SIGN-IN METHOD** tab and activate the **Twitter** option as shown in the following screenshot:

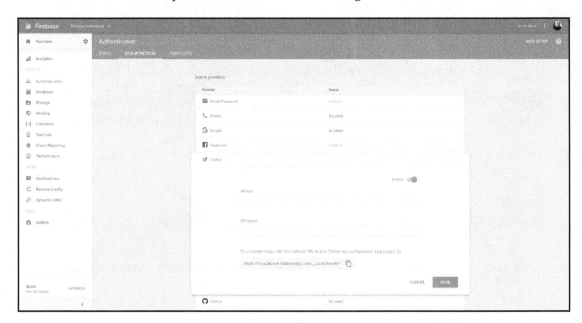

Figure 11: Activating Twitter authentication from the Firebase project console

Now, we will need to create a Twitter application so we can get the app key and secret.

To create a Twitter application, please head to `https://apps.twitter.com/` and create your Twitter application. Once done, head to the **Keys and Access tokens** section and grab the key and secret from there. Then simply copy and paste them to your Firebase console.

How to do it...

1. On the authentication page we created, we now have the following options:

Figure 12: Adding a Twitter authentication button

2. Now let's wire everything up with our JavaScript code, as shown in the following code:

```
let twitterLogin =
document.getElementById('twitterLogin');
twitterLogin.addEventListener('click', () => {
    //TODO: Add Logic here.
});
```

3. Before we move anywhere, we need to configure the `twitterProvider` object by using the following code line:

```
var twitterProvider = new
firebase.auth.TwitterAuthProvider();
```

4. Now, let's exploit the Firebase authentication API calling with the help of the following code block:

```
firebase.auth().signInWithPopup(
 twitterProvider).then(function
(result) {
 console.log(result);
}).catch(function (error) {
 // Handle Errors here.
});
```

Now, your overall code will look similar to this:

```
let twitterLogin =
 document.getElementById('twitterLogin');
twitterLogin.addEventListener('click', () => {
    //1. Get a TwitterAuthProvider instance.
    var twitterProvider = new
    firebase.auth.TwitterAuthProvider();
  firebase.auth().signInWithPopup(
   twitterProvider).then(function
(result) {
      console.log(result);
      var user = result.profile;
    }).catch(function (error) {
    // TODO: Handle Errors.
    });
});
```

After clicking on the button, we will receive the following result:

Figure 13: Authorizing our application using a Twitter account

This window will now ask us to authorize the application using our Twitter account. With this, we'll be able to extract all the required information from the image to all the profile information we can possibly find on the Twitter profile. All you need to do now is find the most suitable way to exploit this and use it with your application.

Implementing Google Sign-in

Google mails, or simply Gmail, accounts are widely used nowadays. This is also one of the most prominent authentication methods for a large number of websites and mobile apps, as it uses the secure Google authentication system to make the secure authentication happen. It's fast, reliable, and can be a source of basic metadata for account creation. In this recipe, we're going to see how we can configure and implement Google Sign-in authentication within our application.

Getting ready

Before we write any code, we need to configure our application to host the Google Sign-in functionality within our Firebase console. To do this, you need to head to Firebase **Console | Authentication | SIGN-IN METHOD** and activate the **Google** option (*Figure 14*):

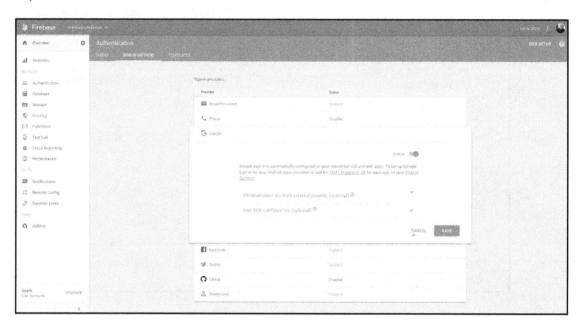

Figure 14: Activating Google authentication from the Firebase Project Console

Since Firebase is now integrated with the Google cloud console, Google authentication, once enabled, will be automatically configured. This means that we don't need to create a Google Sign-in application and configure it accordingly, which actually means that we can use it directly.

How to do it...

1. For our application, we've already created a new connection button and configured its reference on the JavaScript side. The screen after configuring the Google Sign-in button (*Figure 15*):

Figure 15: Adding the Google authentication button for our basic application

2. Now, with the help of the JavaScript code of our application, let's wire up the **Sign in with Google** button for our usage. The code to do this is as follows:

```
let googleLogin =
document.getElementById('googleLogin');
googleLogin.addEventListener('click', () => {
    //TODO: Handle Google authentication here.
});
```

3. Like the rest of the authentication methods, we need to first create an authentication provider object, as shown in the following code block:

```
var googleProvider = new
firebase.auth.GoogleAuthProvider();
```

4. Next, let's use the provider object we just configured and call the Firebase authentication API:

```
firebase.auth().signInWithPopup(
googleProvider).then(function(result) {
    console.log(result);
```

```
     var user = result.user;
}).catch(function (error) {
  //TODO: Handle Errors here.
});
```

5. Now, the overall call will look as follows:

```
let googleLogin =
 document.getElementById('googleLogin');
 googleLogin.addEventListener('click', () => {
   //1. Get a TwitterAuthProvider instance.
   var googleProvider = new
   firebase.auth.GoogleAuthProvider();
   firebase.auth().signInWithPopup(
   googleProvider).then(function(result) {
       console.log(result);
       var user = result.user;
   }).catch(function (error) {
       //TODO: Handle Errors here.
       console.log(error);
   });
});
```

6. After clicking the **Login** button, a new modal popup will be shown. Pick the account you want to use. Once that is done, we will then have the connected user profile, which contains the basic profile and the required tokens for our needs.

How it works...

In order to connect using a Google account with the new Firebase, we don't require anything more than the creation of a Google cloud console application and the grabbing back of the required information. The interconnection and migration between Firebase and Google cloud console make it much simpler for us. All you need to do is activate the options and use the API in order to connect.

Implementing user metadata retrieval

In many cases, having a user dashboard populated with the user's profile information is the way to go. This works well, especially if you have a Firebase-powered business application. The Firebase auth API offers an easy way to retrieve the currently authenticated user's metadata information, and in this recipe, we're going to see how we can do just that.

How to do it...

1. In the authentication section within your code, exploit the `currentUser()` function, as shown in the following code block:

```
var user = firebase.auth().currentUser;
var currentUser = {};
if (user != null) {
  currentUser.name = user.displayName;
  currentUser.email = user.email;
  currentUser.photoUrl = user.photoURL;
  currentUser.emailVerified = user.emailVerified;
  currentUser.uid = user.uid;
}
```

With this, we can get the current user information and use it for our needs.

How it works...

In order to get the user metadata, the user needs to be fully authenticated. Therefore, the `currentUser` object represents the current fully authenticated user.

To do this, we get the `user` object and check that the value is not null. If it is null, it would mean that we don't have any user currently authenticated in the application. If it is not null, we will get the details of our user and can exploit the different metadata related to the connected user.

Implementing the linking of multiple authentication providers

Let's suppose the following: a user created a new profile with email/password authentication, then they filled in their profile information to be saved their profile, and then the operation was performed. But what will happen once they log out and want to log back in again, and find that OAuth button on the login screen? The normal behavior is that they will simply want to use the different OAuth-based authentication methods instead of adding their email/password again.

Choosing one of the many present OAuth authentication options will result in a problem. A new account will be automatically created, and that means more work for the user. From here, we come to the idea of linking multiple accounts into one.

This means that a given user will link all their OAuth authentication profiles into one. This would imply that if they ever wanted to use another method of authentication, they will find themselves logged in to the very same account that they had created the first time.

In this recipe, we're going to see how we can link a current account with social authentication methods.

How to do it...

Let's suppose we have the user profile settings page, with a section for linking those accounts. Now, we will need to do the following:

1. Create a provider object for each supported authentication method as shown in the following code block:

```
let facebookProvider = new
firebase.</span>auth.FacebookAuthProvider();
let twitterProvider  = new
firebase.auth.TwitterAuthProvider();
let googleProvider = new
firebase.auth.GoogleAuthProvider();
```

2. Use the Firebase authentication API call, using the linkWithPopup() function and the provider of our choice, as shown in the following code:

```
auth.currentUser.linkWithPopup(<wanted-
Provider>).then(function(result) {
  //TODO: Handle success response.
}).catch(function(error) {
  //TODO: Handle error response.
});
```

How it works...

Linking accounts makes it easy for users to simply add their different social accounts to one unified account. The logic behind it is quite simple once you start to think about it. The API will do the following tasks:

1. Authenticate you with the social media profile of your choice.
2. Grab and save the authenticated profile and required UIDs, and then save them in your Firebase user account.

5
Securing Application Flow with Firebase Rules

In this chapter, we're going to cover the following recipes:

- Configuring the Firebase Bolt language compiler
- Configuring database data security rules
- Configuring database user data security rules
- Configuring storage files security rules
- Configuring user storage files security rules

Introduction

In modern applications, providing a well-built authentication system is a good thing for any application, but securing the actual resources we have means securing who has access to what, or who can see what. This is essential because we really want only the people with a subscription to have access to, for example, the `Packtpub` library of awesome content. Furthermore, such behavior is now the standard unless your application is a Floppy Bird where it's open to everyone.

Firebase does have, in fact, a powerful authorization system spread with application diverse section, from Storage to Real-time Database. The actual knowledge of how to effectively and successfully handle our authorization system will make our application more secure and give the feel of resilience to its users.

Before starting, it's essential to know how Firebase really performs or applies such security schemes and what languages are required to activate the authorization part. To make everything easy, Firebase has something called the **Bolt language**.

In this chapter, we're going to see how we can get around the powerful Firebase authorization system in juicy recipes, so let's start!

Configuring the Firebase Bolt language compiler

The Firebase team made it clear, we want a more robust system that can be manipulated locally and can be robust enough and more developer friendly, so they created the Bolt language, and according to the Firebase team the language is:

> *"The Bolt language is meant to be used as a convenient frontend to the existing Firebase JSON-based rules language."*

To use it locally, we need to install a NodeJS utility on our development machine, fire up your terminal/cmd, and type the following command:

```
~> npm install -g firebase-bolt
```

This command will go and install the Firebase Bolt compiler locally, now go ahead and create a new file and name it whatever you want, but don't forget to give it the `.bolt` extension.

Now in order to compile this file simply type the following command in your terminal/cmd:

```
~> firebase-bolt <your-file-name>.bolt
```

This will end up by generating a new `.json` file with the Firebase rules language interpretation of the Bolt rules you've added.

Configuring database data security rules

Securing our database is a highly essential thing to do while launching or even while testing your application, simply because we don't want any unwanted behavior to come in place or more, we don't want any security breaches to happen. In this recipe, we're going to see how we can properly secure our Firebase database.

Getting ready

Before starting with this recipe, please make sure that your system is fully configured to support the Bolt language.

How to do it...

To keep things real, let's suppose we're working on our awesome next-gen blogging platform within this platform, so basically, I want to make all my posts available to the public. To do so using the Firebase Bolt language, all I have to do is this:

```
path /articles {
  read() {
      true
  }
  write() {
      isLoggedIn()
  }
}
type Article {
  title: ArticleTitle
  Content : ArticleContent
  Author : currentUser()
}
type ArticleTitle extends String {
  validate() {
  this.length > 0 && this.length <= 200
  }
}
type ArticleContent extends String {
  validate() {
  this.length > 0 && this.length <= 1000
  }
}
currentUser() { auth.uid }
isLoggedIn() { auth != null }
```

How it works...

Let's explain what just happened in the preceding Bolt rules:

1. We're securing the path of the article, making the resources available for the public to read, but in order to write, you will need to be logged in, which means you need to be authenticated. The `isLoggedIn()` function makes sure of that by testing that the global auth variable is not null.

2. We're creating the article type, the article type has a title, content, those types are validated for length, plus an author field that represents the currently authenticated user `uid`.

Configuring database user data security rules

Sometimes or often, we save some user-related data, which means data that has a relationship with a particular user, and in this recipe, we're going to see how we implement just that!

Getting ready

Before starting with this recipe, please make sure that your system is fully configured to support the Bolt language.

How to do it...

Now, let's see how we can secure the set of articles that belong to a specific user:

```
path /articles/{uid}/drafts {
  /create {
    create() { isCreator(uid) }
  }
  /publish {
    update() { isCreator(uid) }
  }
  /delete {
    delete() { isCreator(uid) }
  }
}
```

```
isCreator(uid) { uid == auth.uid }
```

How it works...

Let's discuss the black magic we just created!

1. We're setting a new path for our Articles awesome website in the drafts section for a specific user, represented in the `uid` dynamically changed value.
2. Under that specific path or route, we're securing the sub-routes and check the create, public, and delete routes by checking that the currently authenticated user `uid` is the same as the one who is to manipulate that data within our database.
3. We're setting the `isCreator` function with `uid` as a parameter for privileges checking.

Configuring storage files security rules

File upload service or Firebase Storage service security is highly essential, which means that we don't want any security breaches that can simply delete our file storage or jeopardize the good presence of our files. In this recipe, we're going to see how we can implement/configure our storage security.

Getting ready

In order to secure the Firebase Cloud files, we will need to use the Firebase security rules for Cloud Storage, those rules will be declared to maintain who has access to what, also those rules will define how data is structured and how metadata is saved.

This means that we're going to use a different language then the Bolt one. Also, for these rules to work, please go to your Firebase Project Console | **Storage** section | **RULES** tab and add them from within the presented section as shown in the following screenshot:

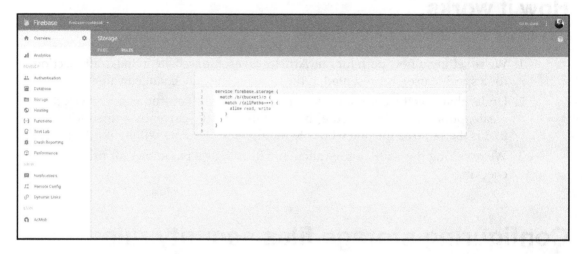

Figure 1: Firebase Storage Rules section.

Within this section, we define the overall security rules that we're going to introduce in this recipe.

How to do it...

Let' suppose we have a two-case scenario, the first one is open to the public and the second one will be available for authenticated users only, so let's see how we can secure them:

```
service firebase.storage {
  match /b/{bucket}/o {
    match /catgifs {
      match /{allGifs=**} {
        allow read;
      }
      match /secret/superfunny/{imageId} {
        allow read, write: if request.auth != null;
      }
    }
  }
}
```

How it works...

So let's explain what we just wrote in the previous rules, line by line so we can understand the Firebase Storage Security rules mechanism:

1. `service firebase.storage`: This line is essential; we're simply telling Firebase about the service we're trying to secure, in our case it will be the Firebase/storage service.

2. `match /b/{bucket}/o`: This rule combines another powerful system, we're speaking mainly about the matching system, the Storage Rules uses this keyword to filter through **files path**, and what Firebase calls **wildcards path** also the match system supports nested matching, which is exactly what we're using in this example. Another interesting point is the matching against in this line: `/b/{bucket}/o`, this is simply another match we're evaluating to make sure that we're securing files within the Cloud Storage bucket.

3. We previously spoke about the **wildcards paths.** They are simply a matching pattern, so let's decompose it. The path we're matching against in this case will be the following: `"/catgifs/**"` which means for every single path variation within it we're using another rule, speaking of `allow` which will simply allow whether `read` or `write` operations or both.

4. Over the last match we had, we're making sure that no user will have the writing privileges except the authenticated one, in this case, where we will be using the wildcard--A simple matcher that represent each element id within that resource--represented in `{imageId}` and allowing both read and write in case the sent `request` holds an `auth` property within, besides those objects are global so you don't need to define them.

Configuring user storage files security rules

Many times, our users will have their own files within our system, so securing the data integrity/presence is highly essential. In this recipe, we'll see how we can configure our user-based file storage system.

Getting ready

In order to be ready, you will need to the follow the given steps :

1. Before starting with this recipe, please make sure that your system is fully configured to support the Bolt language.
2. This means that we're going to use a different language then the Bolt one. Also, for these rules to work, please go to your Firebase Project Console | **Storage** section | **RULES** tab and add them there (*Figure 2*):

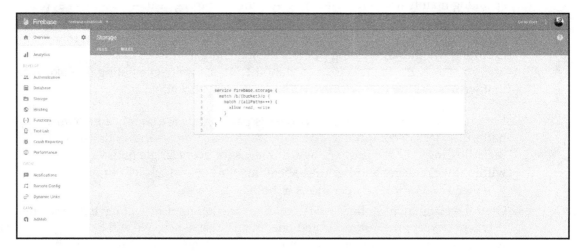

Figure 2: Firebase Storage authorization section.

Within this section, we define the overall security rules that we're going to introduce into these recipes.

How to do it...

Now, let's suppose we have some user-based files that we don't want anyone to read and even write, that is, add a new file to another user personal space, so let's see how we can achieve that:

```
match /secured/personal/{userId}/images/{imageId} {
  allow read: if request.auth.uid == userId;
}
match /secured/personal/{userId}/books/{bookId} {
  allow read: if request.auth.uid == userId;
}
```

```
match /secured/personal/{userId}/images/{imageId} {
  allow write: if request.auth.uid == userId &&
        request.resource.size < 15 * 1024 * 1024 &&
request.resource.contentType.matches('image/.*');
 }
 match /secured/personal/{userId}/books/{bookId} {
   allow write: if request.auth.uid == userId &&
     request.resource.size < 100 * 1024 * 1024 &&
     request.resource.contentType.matches(
     'application/pdf');
 }
```

How it works...

Now let's explain what just happened in the preceding rules:

1. We're trying to protect user-related media, so to do that we've created a new route with two dynamic parameters: the `usersId` for authentication management, and image id as well. In the first two `match` we're using the `allow` rule so we can simply allow the reading of our images and book in case we're authenticated and the request `uid` matched the one from the user asking for them.

2. In the second two-match we're doing some content type management, so if we're securing the images, we need to make sure that images inside that section of the bucket are in fact images and the same thing with books. We're also making some size management, and checking if the image or the book won't exceed the allowed files predefined size.

6
Progressive Applications Powered by Firebase

In this chapter, we'll cover the following recipes:

- Integrating Node-FCM in a NodeJS server
- Implementing service workers
- Implementing sending/receiving registration using Socket.IO
- Implementing sending/receiving registration using post requests
- Receiving web push notification messages
- Implementing custom notification messages

Introduction

One of the newest trends in today's fast-moving web scene is progressive web applications or PWAs for short. Why this trend is in demand is because we have seen a huge jump in the mobile ecosystem, with neat functionalities that combine offline presence, push notification, and installable nature. These functionalities, and many more such functionalities, were rough to relatively impossible to implement in the past, but browser OEMs raised the challenge and progressive web application mindset came to life.

In this chapter, we'll discuss diverse recipes and show what it takes to turn any application into a powerful, fully-optimized progressive web application using Firebase magic. So let's start our journey!

Integrating Node-FCM in a NodeJS server

Keeping in mind that we're in a NodeJS project, we'll see how we can fully integrate the FCM with any Nodejs application. This process is relatively easy and straightforward, and we will see how it can be done in a matter of minutes.

How to do it...

Let's ensure that our working environment is ready for our project, so let's install a couple of dependencies in order to ensure that everything will run smoothly:

1. Open your terminal--in case you are using macOS/Linux--or your cmd--if you're using Windows--and write down the following command:

```
~> npm install fcm-push --save
```

By using this command, we are downloading and installing the `fcm-push` library locally. If this is executed, it will help with managing the process of sending web push notification to our users.

 The NodeJS ecosystem has npm as part of it. So in order to have it on your working machine, you will have to download NodeJS and configure your system within. Here's the official NodeJS link; download and install the suitable version to your system: `https://nodejs.org/en/download/`.

2. Now that we have successfully installed the library locally, in order to integrate it with our applications and start using it, we will just need another line of code. Within your local development project, create a new file that will host the functionality and simply implement the following code:

```
const FCM = require('fcm-push');
```

Congratulations! We're typically done. In subsequent recipes, we'll see how to manage our way through the sending process and how we can successfully send our user's web push notification.

Implementing service workers

Service workers were, in fact, the missing piece in the web scenes of the past. They are what give us the feel of reactivity to any state that a web application, after integrating, can have from, for example, a notification message, an offline-state (no internet connection) and more. In this recipe, we'll see how we can integrate service worker into our application.

Service workers files are event-driven, so everything that will happen inside them will be event based. Since it's JavaScript, we can always hook up listeners to any event. To do that, we will want to give a special logic knowing that if you will use this logic, the event will behave in its default way.

You can read more about service workers and know how you can incorporate them--to achieve numerous awesome features to your application that our book won't cover--from `https://developers.google.com/web/fundamentals/getting-started/primers/service-workers`.

How to do it...

Services workers will live in the browser, so including them within your frontend bundle is the most suitable place for them.

1. Keeping that in mind, let's create a file called `firebase-messaging-sw.js` and `manifest.json` file. The JavaScript file will be our service worker file and will host all major workload, and the JSON file will simply be a metadata config file.

2. After that, ensure that you also create `app.js` file, where this file will be the starting point for our *Authorization* and custom UX. We will look into the importance of each file individually later on, but for now, go back to the `firebase-messaging-sw.js` file and write the following:

```
//[*] Importing Firebase Needed Dependencies
importScripts('https://www.gstatic.com/firebasejs/
3.5.2/firebase-app.js');
importScripts('https://www.gstatic.com/firebasejs/
3.5.2/firebase-messaging.js');

// [*] Firebase Configurations
var config = {
apiKey: "",
authDomain: "",
databaseURL: "",
storageBucket: "",
messagingSenderId: ""
```

```
};
//[*] Initializing our Firebase Application.
firebase.initializeApp(config);

// [*] Initializing the Firebase Messaging Object.
const messaging = firebase.messaging();

// [*] SW Install State Event.
self.addEventListener('install', function(event) {
    console.log("Install Step, let's cache some
    files =D");
  });

// [*] SW Activate State Event.
self.addEventListener('activate', function(event) {
console.log('Activated!', event);});
```

Within any service worker file, the `install` event is always fired first. Within this event, we can handle and add custom logic to any event we want. This can range from saving a local copy of our application in the browser cache to practically anything we want.

3. Inside your metadata file, which will be the `manifest.json` files, write the following line:

```
{
    "name": "Firebase Cookbook",
    "gcm_sender_id": "103953800507"
}
```

How it works...

For this to work, we're doing the following:

1. Importing using `importScripts` while considering this as the script tag with the src attribute in HTML, the firebase app, and the messaging libraries. Then, we're introducing our Firebase config object; we've already discussed where you can grab that object content in the past chapters.
2. Initializing our Firebase app with our config file.
3. Creating a new reference from the `firebase.messaging` library--always remember that everything in Firebase starts with a reference.
4. We're listening to the `install` and `activate` events and printing some `stdout` friendly message to the browser debugger.

Also, within our `manifest.json` file, we're adding the following metadata:

1. The application name (optional).
2. The `gcm_sender_id` with the given value. Keep in mind that this value will not change for any new project you have or will create in the future.

> The `gcm_sender_id` added line might get deprecated in the future, so keep an eye on that.

Implementing sending/receiving registration using Socket.IO

By now, we've integrated our FCM server and made our service worker ready to host our awesome custom logic. Like we mentioned, we're about to send web push notifications to our users to expand and enlarge their experience without application. Lately, web push notification is being considered as an engagement feature that any cool application nowadays, ranging from Facebook and Twitter to numerous e-commerce sites, is making good use of. So in the first approach, let's see how we can make it happen with Socket.IO.

In order to make the FCM server aware of any client--basically, a browser--Browser OEM has what we call a `registration_id`. This token is a unique token for every browser that will represent our clients by their browsers and needs to be sent to the FCM server.

> Each browser generates its own `registration_id` token. So if your user uses, for instance, chrome for their first interaction with the server and they used firefox for their second experience, the web push notification message won't be sent, and they need to send another token so that they can be notified.

How to do it...

1. Now, go back to your NodeJS project that was created in the first recipe. Let's download the `node.js socket.io` dependency:

```
~> npm install express socket.io --save
```

2. `Socket.io` is also event-based and lets us create our custom event for everything we have, plus some native one for connections. Also, we've installed ExpressJS for configuration sake in order to create a `socket.io` server.

3. Now after doing that, we need to configure our `socket.io` server using `express`. In this case, do as shown in the following code:

```
const express = require('express');
const app = express();
app.io = require('socket.io')();

// [*] Configuring our static files.
app.use(express.static('public/'));

// [*] Configuring Routes.
app.get('/', (req, res) => {
    res.sendFile(__dirname + '/public/index.html');
});

// [*] Configuring our Socket Connection.
app.io.on('connection', socket => {
 console.log('Huston ! we have a new connection
    ...');
})
```

So let's discuss the preceding code, where we are simply doing the following:

- Importing express and creating a new express app.
- Using the power of object on the fly, we've included the `socket.io` package over a new sub-object over the express application. This integration makes our express application now support the usage of `socket.io` over the Application.
- We're indicating that we want to use the public folder as our static files folder, which will host our HTML/CSS/Javascript/IMG resources.
- We're listening to the `connection`, which will be fired once we have a new upcoming client.
- Once a new connection is up, we're printing a friendly message over our console.

4. Let's configure our frontend. Head directly to your `index.html` files located in the public folder, and add the following line at the head of your page:

```
<script src="/socket.io/socket.io.js"></script>
```

5. The `socket.io.js` file will be served in application launch time, so don't worry much if you don't have one locally. Then, at the bottom of our `index.html` file before the closing of our `<body>` tag, add the following:

```
<script>
   var socket = io.connect('localhost:3000');
</script>
```

In the preceding script, we're connecting our frontend to our `socket.io` backend. Supposedly, our server is in port `3000`; this way, we ensured that our two applications are running in sync.

6. Head to your `app.js` files--created in the earlier recipes; create and import it if you didn't do so already--and introduce the following:

```
//[*] Importing Firebase Needed Dependencies
importScripts('https://www.gstatic.com/firebasejs/
   3.5.2/firebase-app.js');
importScripts('https://www.gstatic.com/firebasejs/
   3.5.2/firebase-messaging.js');

// [*] Firebase Configurations
var config = {
  apiKey: "",
  authDomain: "",
  databaseURL: "",
  storageBucket: "",
  messagingSenderId: ""
};
//[*] Initializing our Firebase Application.
firebase.initializeApp(config);

// [*] Initializing the Firebase Messaging Object.
const messaging = firebase.messaging();
```

Everything is great; don't forget to import the `app.js` file within your `index.html` file. We will now see how we can grab our `registration_id` token next:

1. As I explained earlier, the registration token is unique per browser. However, in order to get it, you should know that this token is considered a privacy issue. To ensure that they do not fall into the wrong hands, it's not available everywhere and to get it, you need to ask for the **Browser User Permission**. Since you can use it in any particular application, let's see how we can do that.

The registration_id token will be considered as security and privacy threat to the user in case this token has been compromised, because once the attacker or the hacker gets the tokens, they can send or spam users with push messages that might have a malicious intent within, so safely keeping and saving those tokens is a priority.

2. Now, within your `app.js` files that we created early on, let's add the following lines of code underneath the Firebase messaging reference:

```
messaging.requestPermission()
    .then(() => {
        console.log("We have permission !");
        return messaging.getToken();
    })
    .then((token) => {
        console.log(token);
        socket.emit("new_user", token);
    })
    .catch(function(err) {
     console.log("Huston we have a problem !",err);
    });
```

We've sent out token using the awesome feature of `socket.io`. In order to get it now, let's simply listen to the same event and hope that we will get some data over our NodeJS backend. We will now proceed to learn about receiving registration token:

1. Back to the `app.js` file, inside our `connection` event, let's add the following code:

```
socket.on('new_user', (endpoint) => {
  console.log(endpoint);
  //TODO : Add endpoint aka.registration_token, to
  secure place.
 });
```

2. Our `socket.io` logic will look pretty much as shown in the following code block:

```
// [*] Configuring our Socket Connection.
app.io.on('connection', socket => {
    console.log('Huston ! we have a new connection
        ...');
    socket.on('new_user', (endpoint) => {
        console.log(endpoint);
    //TODO : Add endpoint aka.registration_token, to
        secure place.
```

```
    });
  });
```

Now, we have our bidirectional connection set. Let's grab that `regitration_token` and save it somewhere safe for further use.

How it works...

In the first part of the recipe, we did the following:

1. Importing using `importScripts` considering it a script tag with src attribute in HTML, the firebase app, and messaging libraries. Then, we're introducing our Firebase Config object. We've already discussed where you can grab that object content in the previous chapters.
2. Initializing our Firebase app with our config file.
3. Creating a new reference from `firebase.messaging` library--always remember that everything in Firebase starts with a reference.

Let's discuss what we did previously in the section where we talked about getting the `registration_token` value:

1. We're using the Firebase messaging reference that we created earlier and executing the `requestPermission()` function, which returns a promise.
2. Next--assuming that you're following along with this recipe--you will do the following over your page. After launching the development server, you will get a request from your page (*Figure 1*):

Figure 1: Notification authorization request

3. Now, let's get back to the code. If we allow the notification, the promise resolver will be executed and then we will return the `registration_token` value from `themessaging.getToken()`.

4. Then, we're sending that token over a socket and emitting that with an even name of `new_user`.

 `Socket.io` uses web sockets and like we explained before, sockets are event based. So in order to have a two-way connection between nodes, we need to `emit`, that is, send an event after giving it a name and listening to the same event with that name.

Remember the `socket.io` event's name because we'll incorporate that into our further recipes.

Implementing sending/receiving registration using post requests

In a different approach from the one used in `Socket.io`, let's explore the other way around using post requests. This means that we'll use a REST API that will handle all that for us. At the same time, it will handle saving the `registration_token` value in a secure place as well. So let's see how we can configure that.

How to do it...

1. First, let's start writing our REST API. We will do that by creating an express post endpoint. This endpoint will be porting our data to the server, but before that, let's install some dependencies using the following line:

```
~> npm install express body-parser --save
```

Let's discuss what we just did:

- We're using npm to download ExpressJS locally to our development directory.
- Also, we're downloading body-parser. This is an ExpressJS middleware that will host all post requests data underneath the `body` subobject. This module is quite a common package in the NodeJS community, and you will find it pretty much everywhere.

2. Now, let's configure our application. Head to the `app.js` file and add the following code lines there:

```
const express = require('express');
const app = express();
const bodyParser = require('body-parser');

// [*] Configuring Body Parser.
app.use(bodyParser.json());

// [*] Configuring Routes.
app.post('/regtoken', (req, res) => {
  let reg_token =req.body.regtoken;
  console.log(reg_token);
  //TODO : Create magic while saving this token in
    secure place.
});
```

In the preceding code, we're doing the following:

- Importing our dependencies including ExpressJS and BodyParser.
- In the second step, we're registering the body parser middleware. You can read more about body parser and how to properly configure it to suit your needs from `https://github.com/expressjs/body-parser`.
- Next, we're creating an express endpoint or a route. This route will host our custom logic to manage the retrieval of the registration token sent from our users.

3. Now, let's see how we can send the registration token to form our user's side. In this step, you're free to use any HTTP client you seek. However, in order to keep things stable, we'll use the browser native fetch APIs.

4. Since we've managed to fully configure our routes, it can host the functionality we want. Let's see how we can get the `registration_token` value and send it to our server using post request and the native browser HTTP client named `fetch`:

```
messaging.requestPermission()
  .then(() => {
      console.log("We have permission !");
      return messaging.getToken();
  })
  .then((token) => {
    console.log(token);
    //[*] Sending the token
    fetch("http://localhost:3000/regtoken", {
      method: "POST"
```

```
        }).then((resp) => {
            //[*] Handle Server Response.
        })
        .catch(function(err) {
            //[*] Handle Server Error.
        })
    })
    .catch(function(err) {
        console.log("Huston we have a problem !", err);
    });
```

How it works...

Let's discuss what we just wrote in the preceding code:

1. We're using the Firebase messaging reference that we created earlier and executing the `requestPermission()` function that returns a promise.

2. Next, supposing that you're following along with this recipe, after launching the development server you will get the following authorization request from your page:

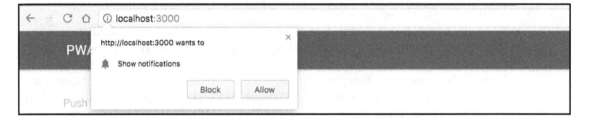

Figure 2: Application Notification authorization request

3. Moving back to the code, if we allow the notification, the promise resolver will be executed and then we will return the `registration_token` value from the `messaging.getToken()`.

4. Next, we're using the `Fetch` API given it a URL as a first parameter and a method name that is `post` and handling the response and error.

Since we saw the different approaches to exchange data between the client and the server, in the next recipe, we will see how we can receive web push notification messages from the server.

Receiving web push notification messages

We can definitely say that things are on a good path. We managed to configure our message to the server in the past recipes. Now, let's work on getting the message back from the server in a web push message. This is a proven way to gain more leads and regain old users. It is a sure way to re-engage your users, and success stories do not lie. Facebook, Twitter, and e-commerce websites are the living truth on how a web push message can make a difference in your ecosystem and your application in general.

How to do it...

Let's see how we can unleash the power of push messages. The API is simple and the way to do has never been easier, so let's how we can do that!

1. Let's write down the following code over our `firebase-messaging-sw.js` file:

```
// [*] Special object let us handle our Background Push
   Notifications
messaging.setBackgroundMessageHandler(function(payload)
   { return
self.registration.showNotification(payload.data.title,
      body: payload.data.body);
   });
```

Let's explain the preceding code:

- We're using the already created messaging object created using the Firebase messaging library, and we're calling.
  the `setBackgroundMessageHandler()` function. This will mean that we will catch all the messages that we will keep receiving in the background.
- We're using the service worker object represented in the self-object, and we're calling the `showNotification()` function and passing it some parameters. The first parameter is the title, and we're grabbing it from the server; we'll see how we can get it in just a second. The second parameter is the body of the message.

2. Now, we've prepared our frontend to received messages. Let's send them from the server, and we will see how we can do that using the following code:

```
var fcm = new FCM('<FCM_CODE>');
var message = {
    to: data.endpoint, // required fill with device
      token or topics
    notification: {
        title: data.payload.title,
        body: data.payload.body
    }
};
    fcm.send(message)
  .then(function(response) {
 console.log("Successfully sent with response: ",
    response);
  })
  .catch(function(err) {
      console.log("Something has gone wrong!");
      console.error(err);
  })
});
```

3. The most important part is `FCM_CODE`. You can grab it in the Firebase console by going to the Firebase Project **Console** and clicking on the **Overview** tab (*Figure 3*):

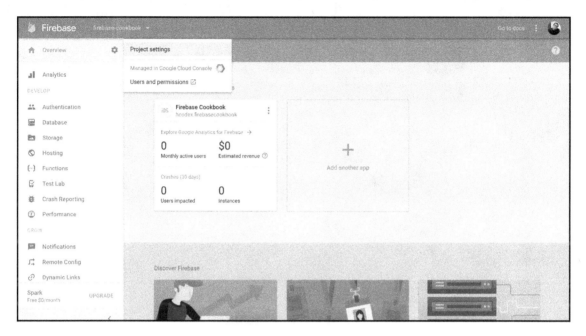

Figure 3: Getting the project FCM_CODE

4. Then, go to the **CLOUD MESSAGING** tab and copy and paste the **Server Key** in the section (*Figure 4*):

Figure 4: Getting the Server Keycode

How it works...

Now, let's discuss the code that what we just wrote:

1. The preceding code can be put everywhere, which means that you can send push notifications in every part of your application.

2. We're composing our notification message by putting the registration token and the information we want to send.

3. We're using the `fcm.send()` method in order to send our notification to the wanted users.

Congratulations! We're done; now go and test your awesome new functionality!

Implementing custom notification messages

In the previous recipes, we saw how we can send a normal notification. Let's add some controllers and also learn how to add some pictures to it so that we can prettify it a bit.

How to do it...

1. Now write the following code and add it to our earlier code over the messaging.setBackgroundMessageHandler() function. So, the end result will look something like this:

```
// [*] Special object let us handle our Background
      Push Notifications
messaging.setBackgroundMessageHandler(function(payload)
  {
    const notificationOptions = {
        body: payload.data.msg,
        icon: "images/icon.jpg",
        actions: [
            {
                action : 'like',
                title: 'Like',
                image: '<link-to-like-img>'
            },
            {
                action : 'dislike',
                title: 'Dislike',
                image: '<link-to-like-img>'
            }
        ]
    }
    self.addEventListener('notificationclick',
        function(event) {
        var messageId = event.notification.data;
        event.notification.close();
        if (event.action === 'like') {
    console.log("Going to like something !");
        } else if (event.action === 'dislike') {
    console.log("Going to dislike something !");
        } else {
    console.log("wh00t !");
        }
    }, false);
    return
```

```
self.registration.showNotification(
payload.data.title,notificationOptions);
});
```

How it works...

Let's discuss what we've done so far:

1. We added the `notificationOptions` object that hosts some of the required metadata, such as the body of the message and the image. Also, in this case, we're adding actions, which means we'll add custom buttons to our notification message. These will range from `title` to `image`, the most important part is the `action` name.

2. Next, we listened on `notificationclick`, which will be fired each time one of the actions will be selected. Remember the `action` field we added early on; it'll be the differentiation point between all actions we might add.

3. Then, we returned the notification and showed it using the `showNotification()` function.

7
Firebase Admin SDK

In this chapter, we'll cover the following recipes:

- Integrating the Firebase Admin SDK
- Implementing user account management by fetching users
- Implementing user account management by creating accounts
- Implementing user account management by deleting accounts
- Implementing notification sending

Introduction

The Firebase Admin SDK provides more power than the existing power you have by offering privileged access to a different section in your console. From sending a notification to having the power to manipulate the user accounts, it also manipulates the Realtime Database and manages security via token generation and verification. It's the most suitable solution for application admin dashboards that can be applicable today.

This SDK is available in different ecosystems from NodeJS to Java and also over Python, with different implementation levels. The knowledge of using NodeJS can give us ultimate access to all the supported functionalities, which is not the case for other ecosystems. That's exactly what we'll work with; we'll use the Firebase Admin SDK in NodeJS context.

In this chapter, we'll see how we can manage our way through the SDK and create some awesome new functionalities that will help us extend the existing power of our application.

Integrating the Firebase Admin SDK

Within this recipe, we're going to cover how to integrate Firebase Admin SDK with our project. The steps are intuitive and quite simple as any other integration within Firebase, so let's get to it.

Getting ready

Since we'll use the Firebase Admin SDK NodeJS client, we need to ensure that NodeJS is present in our development system, so first head directly to `nodejs.org/download` and download the suitable version for your system.

How to do it...

After doing so, let's ensure that we have NodeJS present in our system; head directly to your system and write the following command:

```
~> node --version
```

Typically, if everything went okay, you will be prompted with the NodeJS version present on your development machine.

Next, create the working directly, transit to it, and write the following command, initializing your project to be a NodeJS application:

```
~> npm init
```

Follow the steps, writing the metadata that you want your project to have, or simply click on return/enter; the `package.json` file is finally created.

Next, let's simply download the SDK and incorporate it into our project; in your terminal, write the following command:

```
~> npm i firebase-admin --save
```

This command will go to download the Firebase Admin SDK and its dependencies locally.

Next, let's head directly to our Firebase **Console**, in the **Overview** | **SERVICE ACCOUNTS** (*Figure 1*):

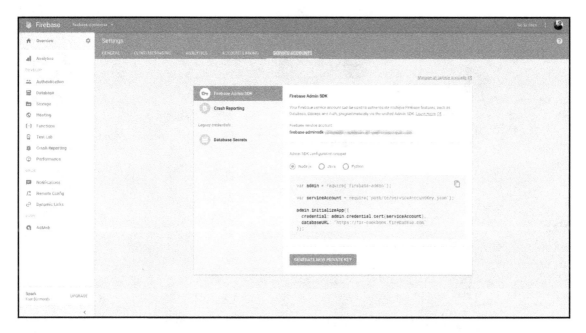

Figure 1: Getting the Firebase Admin SDK configuration

Now click on the **GENERATE NEW PRIVATE KEY** button, and you will be greeted with the following modal (*Figure 2*):

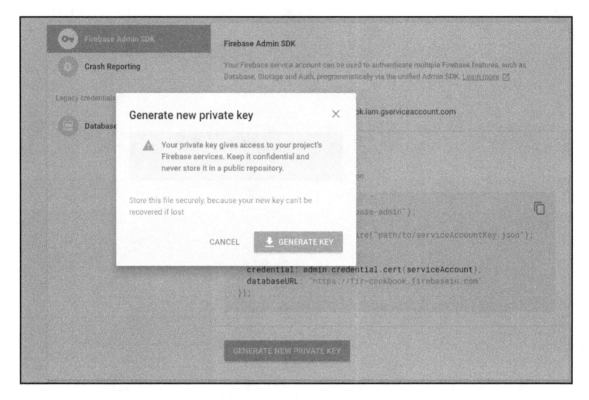

Figure 2: Generating and the Getting the Private key file

Next, click on the **GENERATE KEY** button to download the secure JSON file.

This file will have the required information to perform privileged and secure connection to your Admin section within your Firebase Project; it will have the `project_id`, `private_key`, and other encryption metadata that will secure the connection.

Keep this file in a secure place; don't ship and don't make it public, because it contains information that you will use in order to connect in a secure way and perform a privileged action against your users, data, notification sending, and more. So, keeping it in a secure location is a high-priority action.

Next, simply copy/paste the snippet provided by Firebase in order to start using the Firebase Admin SDK in your local development directory, and you're good to go.

Implementing user account management by fetching users

The Admin SDK is present to provide one of the advanced features of Firebase within the same scope and perspective of better handling and better experience. Managing user accounts will include functionalities such as creating/deleting users, fetching users by email ID or phone number, updating users account properties, and accessing metadata.

In this recipe, we'll see how we can fetch users using nothing but the Firebase Admin NodeJS library. So, let's get busy!

How to do it...

Fetching users is the most common feature that any platform would want to feature, so let's see how we can fetch users from their email and phone number.

We will first learn about fetching users by email:

1. Open up your project that we've created and configured already. Let's add the following line to see how we can fetch users by email.
2. Let's suppose we've got a search input and a button; this will finally send a post request to our NodeJS backend, so we can now access our post request body using BodyParser:

```
req.post('/users/search/email', (req, res) => {
  let email = req.body.email;
   admin.auth().getUserByEmail(email)
     .then(users => {
        //[*] TODO: properly the User.
   })
   .catch(err => {
   logger.error(`[*] Huston we've an error:
    Error over getting users by email, with error:
    ${error}`)
      res.json({
    message: `External Error: getting user by email,
     error : ${error}`
      })
```

```
          })
      })
```

With this, typically we're done; all you need is to properly handle the user recovering from the API and properly showcase it.

Next in line is fetching users by phone number, which we will now take a look at:

1. As with phone number searching, you will need a properly configured project to run the query. Now simply create your endpoint, supposing that the phone number will be sent via a post-quest. It will be grabbed using BodyParser and injected into the request body object.
2. Now, simply write the following code:

```
req.post('/users/search/phone', (req, res) => {
  let phoneNumber = req.body.phone;
  admin.auth().getUserByPhoneNumber(phoneNumber)
    .then(users => {
      //[*] TODO: properly the User.
    })
    .catch(err => {
    logger.error(`[*] Huston we've an error: Error over
    getting users by phone number, with error: ${err}`)
    res.json({message: `External Error: getting user by phone
      number, error : ${err}`})
    })
})
```

All you need is to properly handle the sending/showcasing of the user.

Congratulations! You've successfully configured your dashboard to grab users using both email and phone numbers.

Implementing user account management by creating accounts

Using nothing but the Firebase SDK, we can create new accounts with some metadata directly from our dashboard so let's see how we can make that happen.

Getting ready

To perform such an operation, you will probably need to have a form; such a form will have many fields, including, but not exclusively, the email, password, name, and more. Such a form will perform a post request in order to send the data from our frontend to our backend, also known as API. Now over in our API, let's create a new route and add the custom logic that will eventually handle such a request.

How to do it...

Within our example, we'll have an express server running which will give us the possibility to have some basic routes that we'll use in order to create our dashboard, and what needed now is to have a route that will help us create a user, so let's see how to implement that.

```
req.post('/create/users', (req, res) => {
    let {email, password, fullName, image} = req.body;
    admin.auth().createUser({
email : email,
password: password, //Must be at least six characters long
        displayName: fullName,
        photoURL: image
    })
    .then(user => {
        //[*] Do something within the response !
    })
    .catch(err => {
        logger.error(`External Error: While creating new
         account, with error : ${err}`);
        res.json({
            message: `Error: while creating new account, with
         error: ${err}`})
        });
    })
})
```

> Firebase already has a set of fields that you will need to respect when you create a new account; that list includes uid, email, password, photoURL, phoneNumber, displayName, and more, and you can find them in the official documentation from https://firebase.google.com/docs/auth/admin/manage-users.

In the preceding code, we're doing the following:

1. Grabbing all the fields from the `req.body` object.
2. Calling the `createUser()` function and adding the user metadata to it.
3. Using the generated promise if resolved means that everything went alright and the account was created, else we will find the generated error within the Catch section so you can handle it properly.

Implementing user account management by deleting accounts

In order to delete an account, the Firebase Admin SDK will require you to have the user UID; such an ID can be grabbed in different ways, but one of the functionalities we have seen is for users to delete their own account, so this utility can be helpful. Let's see how we can make it happen.

Getting ready

In the user dashboard or settings pages, we want users to have a button to delete their accounts; this will launch a `post` request to our backend, calling the API to delete the account. This final should be secure enough to host such a functionality.

How to do it...

Let's create our API and implement the Admin SDK delete functionality:

```
req.post('/users/:uid/delete', (req, res) => {
    admin.auth().deleteUser(req.params.uid)
        .then(() => {
    //[*] Response is empty if everything went OK !
        })
    .catch(err => {
    logger.error(`External Error: While deleting user
      account, with ${req.params.uid}, & with error :
      ${err}`);
        res.json({
    message: `Error: while deleting your account,
      with error: ${err}`});
        });
```

```
    })
```

Typically, we're done; all you need is to do is properly handle the response from the backend, which should be blank, or if not, handle the shown error.

How it works...

In the preceding code, we built our Admin dashboard and defined a diverse call to our Firebase instance. All those operations depend on the presence of a user UID; it's the unique user identifier that we need to pass with each function call.

Implementing notification sending

In `Chapter 6`, *Progressive Applications powered by Firebase,* we introduced how we can integrate the old FCM utility within our NodeJS server. Now the Firebase SDK provides us with more diverse methods to send push notification messages; plus, it plays nicely with other services, so let's see how we can send push notifications directly to our users using nothing but the Firebase Admin SDK.

How to do it...

In order to send push notification messages to users, we need to have their `registration_token`; such a token is grabbed from the user browser side, whether it's mobile or desktop. Google Chrome and Mozilla Firefox support this functionality, and at the time of writing this book, Safari included the functionality over nightly build, while MS Edge is still in development. It's all related to whether the Browser OEM support service works or not.

Another way is via native mobile apps; you can retrieve that `registration_token` and send it directly to your Firebase instance in case you have native mobile apps.

 For in-depth information about the retrieval of the `registration_token`, refer to `Chapter 6`, *Progressive Applications powered by Firebase.*

We also want to take a look at a specific scenario here.

Let's imagine that we want to send a statement; this statement usually has a declaration of the new term of services, or something similar. Such a statement requires the approval of the application's users, so the process of sending the notification to all users is essential here. Let's see how we can perform such an operation:

```
req.post('/urgent/policy', (req, res) => {
let registrationTokens = [];
//[*] TODO : Grab the registration_ids from secure
  place.
let payload = {
    notification: {
      title: "Policy changes!",
      body: "Please verify your account, our policy is
      changing"
    }
};
  admin.messaging().sendToDevice(registrationTokens,
   payload)
   .then(resp => {
     //[*] Properly handle the response
   })
   .catch(err => {
      logger.error(`External Error: While sending
    policy push notification, with error : ${err}`);
      res.json({
         message: `Error: while deleting your account,
    with error: ${err}` });
      });
});
```

By now, you've successfully sent your urgent changes to your users; they will get a notification, whether it was via mobile or desktop.

Now let's suppose that you have another scenario. For instance, your users only want to see urgent news from your new application. This is possible using the Firebase topic subscription; it starts with the user subscribing to the topic from their mobile site to a `top_news` topic, and the second part is within your backend, where you only want to grab any major news and send them back to your users.

> In order to know how to perform Firebase topic subscription over your native Android/iOS project, refer to `Chapter 12`, *Hack Application's Growth*.

Now, let's see how we can perform a topic-based notification sending:

```
//[*] TODO : Define the sending manner: typically a
   timer or a scheduler.
let topic = "top_news";
//[*] TODO: Define the message format over payload
   object
let payload = {};
//[*] Instead of registration_ids we send payload to
    a topic.
    admin.messaging().sendToTopic(topic, payload)
    .then(resp => {
        //[*] TODO: Handle response !
    })
    .catch(err => {
     logger.error(`External Error: While sending
    topic push notification, for topic: ${topic},
     with error : ${err}`);
    });
```

How it works...

The steps behind serving those notifications, whether they are based on the topic or standard ones, are similar; so typically, what we're doing for this to work is the following:

1. We're specifying our routes; typically, they will be based on our dashboard routes.
2. We're fetching the overall registration IDs, the one that belongs to and represents a specific client or user within our system, and is unique per user.
3. We're specifying the message payload (content).
4. We're using the Firebase Admin SDK messaging API to send our message to our users, whether it is via a normal message or topic-based sending.

8

Extend Firebase with Cloud Functions

In this chapter, we're going to cover the following recipes:

- Getting started with Cloud Functions
- Implementing data manipulation
- Implementing data-change monitoring
- Welcoming users upon account creation
- Implementing account email confirmation
- Sending re-engagement emails to inactive Firebase users

Introduction

Knowing about Firebase's static capabilities, going the extra mile with it can be difficult, if not impossible, sometimes. However, the Firebase team this year has introduced something that, in my opinion, will change the rules of the game. I'm speaking technically about Firebase Cloud Functions. Cloud Functions is the perfect solution for extending most of the present capabilities of Firebase, from the database to allowing awesome re-engagement for your users. Using Cloud Functions will transform your application from being just backend-less to serverless, with zero maintenance. This means that you are going to perform some magic in order to make sure that your function is behaving with one to endless users. At the same time, you can ensure that they are secure and that their privacy is never jeopardized.

The functions we're going to write will be using some Node.js magic, and it needs a couple of configurations before we start. So let us begin with the Firebase Cloud Functions journey!

 As a golden tip, Packt publishing offer tons of materials both in Book/Video course around NodeJS and, here's a link where you will find al the greatest and finest Books/videos courses around Nodejs hosted by Packt Public Library: `https://www.packtpub.com/all?search=nodejs`.

Getting started with Cloud Functions

In this recipe, we're going to see, step by step, how we can integrate Cloud Functions with our project. We can use this recipe whenever we want to integrate Cloud Functions with a project, so let's get cloudy!

Getting ready

Everything starts from the Firebase CLI, an awesome utility for handling all your Firebase needs.

 For a more precise idea of how to download and install the Firebase Admin SDK onto a development machine, please refer to the `Chapter 7`, *Firebase Admin SDK*.

How to do it...

After we've successfully installed the Firebase CLI, let's see the needed steps in order to get started with Firebase Cloud Functions.

1. Once you've successfully installed the Firebase CLI utility, you will need to initialize your project. To do so, execute the following command:

```
~> firebase init functions
```

2. Then you will need to select the project you want. This would be the project that you want to associate Cloud Functions with, or you can create a new project if you don't have a present one.

3. In my case, I want to create a new project bundled with Cloud Functions, so I will use the following command:

```
~> firebase init
```

4. This time, we will start with the Functions option (*Figure 1*):

Figure: 1: Creating a new Cloud Functions project using the Firebase CLI

5. Now, choose the project you want to associate Cloud Functions with, as follows (*Figure 2*):

Figure 2: Choosing project we want to associate our Firebase Cloud Functions with.

6. Next, you will be prompted with the following screen asking you if you want to download and install the needed dependencies or not, for our needs we will answer with "**Y**" for yes or simply press *Return/Enter* button in your keyboard (*Figure 3*):

Figure 3: Installing project's needed dependencies.

Once npm has finished and the dependencies download, open your project using your favorite code editor, it will look pretty much like this one (*Figure 4*):

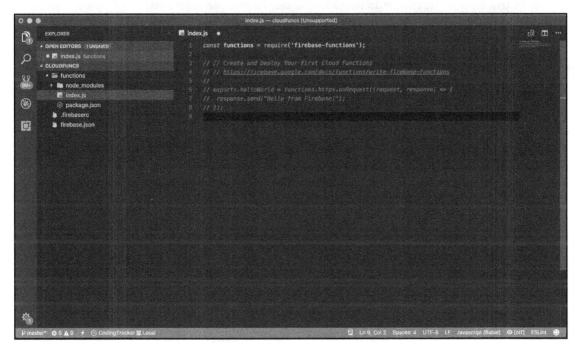

Figure 4: Project structure after successfully Project/Dependencies creation and setup.

And now, we're set to start writing our Cloud Functions!

Implementing data manipulation

The Firebase database is bundled with lots of events, and for our Cloud Functions to function properly we're going to exploit a set of these functions that will make our lives much simpler.

As a use case, we're going to see how we can integrate Firebase Cloud Functions within an Online store. The function job here is to listen to any new-made unfinished purchase and set its status to pending state.

So, let's get to it!

Getting ready

Before you start adding your function's implementation, please make sure that your project is ready for Cloud Functions. For double check, please look at the preceding recipe for help-
-*Getting started with Cloud Functions*.

How to do it...

Once you've successfully configured your project, let's start integrating the function within our online store.

1. We need to listen to our purchases collections over our Database using the onWrite function to any new writing operation that was made over our collection, like the following :

```
exports.updateStats =
 functions.database.ref('/purchases/{pushId}/item').onWrite(event
    =>
   {
    const addedPurchases = event.data.val();
    const status = `${addedPurchases.name.toUpperCase()} - is a
    ${addedPurchases.type} - is PENDING`;
    return event.data.ref.parent.child('status').set(status);
});
```

2. Now to upload your newly created function, simply head to your console and execute the following command:

```
~> firebase deploy --only functions
```

3. Now, whenever somebody tries to make a new purchase, we'll get the following output from our Database (*Figure 5*):

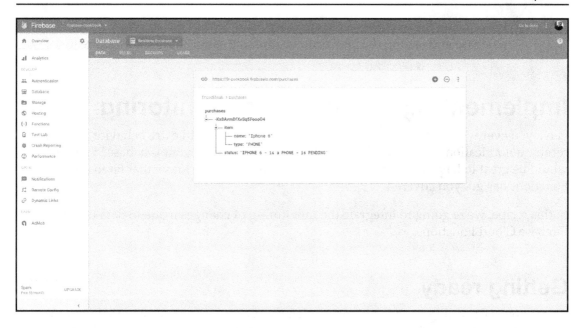

Figure 5: Our pushed data after Cloud Function manipulations.

In case you noticed, the **status** field was not present initially when we pushed the data to our Database, but it was added while the data were being manipulated over the Cloud Function that we've implemented.

How it works...

Let's explain what just happened:

1. We've made a listener over one of our diverse links: `/purchases/{pushId}/item`. The `pushId` function represents the automatically generated ID that Firebase gives to any new field that was introduced using the `push()` method. Also, we're listening to the item element that can be anything you have in your database, but, in the case of my store, any newly purchased item will be over the `item` object.

2. We're retrieving that new field from the event object we've got from Cloud Functions using the `onWrite()` event.

3. We're formalizing the status we want our status object to having.

4. We're using the event object again to navigate within the structure of our database and setting the new status within the same object that was created.

Implementing data-change monitoring

Have you ever wondered what would it be like if you could add extra behavior, or even receive a notification, whenever there's a data manipulation in your database? I bet that would be great to have a feature, and you would be amazed to know that Firebase Cloud Functions has got you covered!

In this recipe, we're going to integrate the monitoring of changes made to data using Firebase Cloud Functions.

Getting ready

Before you start adding your function's implementation, please make sure that your project is ready for Cloud Functions. To double check, please refer to the *Getting started with Cloud Functions* recipe for assistance.

How to do it...

1. As a general use case, we can monitor any path or data we want using nothing but the changed() function, this will return a true value if the data did change. So, let's now learn how we can implement it:

```
exports.updateStats =
 functions.database.ref('/path/to/data').onWrite(
   event => {
   const data = event.data;
   const anotherData = data.child('childPath');
   if(anotherData.changed()) {
       //TODO: implement notification
   } else {
       //return promise.
   }
});
```

It's as simple as that, we can check if our data changed.

How it works...

The idea behind it is very simple. Generally, within our data path, we will have a flag. This flag will be our indicator and will be true if the data changed. So, it will take just one call to check if the data changed and we can implement the notification process accordingly.

Welcoming users upon account creation

Welcoming our users when they create their account is something we would have definitely wanted to do before. But, due to lack of support, it was not possible. Now that we have this facility provided by Firebase, it allows us to have an extra custom backend to welcome users to account creation. In this recipe, we're going to see how we can make that happen!

Getting ready

Before you start adding your function's implementation, please make sure that your project is ready for Cloud Functions.

How to do it...

1. The new version of Firebase is more event-ready than before. This means that now, whenever we create a new account, we are going to have an event. Bear in mind that this functionality needs the super admin authorization that you won't find anywhere besides Cloud Functions and the Admin SDK API.

2. This is how we listen to the account creation event:

```
exports.sendEmailUponAccountCreation =
  functions.auth.user().onCreate(ev => {
    //Getting the new User account informations.
    const newUser = ev.data;
    const email = newUser.email;
    const fullName = newUser.displayName;
    //TODO : Send Email from here
});
```

3. Now, to upload your newly created function simply head to your console and execute the following command:

```
~> firebase deploy --only functions
```

How it works...

Let's digest the preceding code. We're calling for the authentication module, listening to the `user().OnCreate()` function, and then giving it a callback with an event object holding our newly created account information.

What you will have to do next is even simpler--hook your most trusted email service. Now, whether it is a simple Nodemailer or a more interesting paid solution, it's up to you to use the service you prefer.

Implementing account email confirmation

The email confirmation process is one of the most widely spread functionalities over forms and event management applications. Firebase truly shines as it uses such an application, and now with Cloud Functions, we can make the process faster and free of backend code. So, let's see how we can make this happen.

Getting ready

Before you start adding your function's implementation, you will need to complete the extra step and configure your project with Cloud Functions. To do so, just check the *Getting started with Cloud Functions* recipe.

How to do it...

Let's suppose we have a form, and this form will give people the opportunity to register for the date of an upcoming book release. For this, what we will need to do is quite simple:

1. We will listen to any new writing operation that is being made over our form DB route and extract the data accordingly using the following code:

```
exports.sendEmailWhenSubscribe =
functions.database.ref('/bookevent').onWrite(ev =>
```

```
        {
    //getting the event data.
    const userMeta = ev.data;
    const email = userMeta.email;
    const displayName = user.displayName;
    switch(ev.eventType) {
        case
    "providers/firebase.auth/eventTypes/user.create" :
        //TODO Send confirmation email from here
        break;
        case
    "providers/firebase.auth/eventTypes/user.delete" :
        //TODO Send Goodbye email from here
        break;
        ...
        ..
        .
    }
})
```

2. In case you want to deploy your function and test it, head to your terminal of choice and execute the following command:

```
~> firebase deploy --only functions
```

This will upload your function and execute it. Once that is done, it will return an exploitable link that you can use for your needs.

How it works...

Let's discuss what we've written in the preceding code:

1. We're calling for the database reference this time over a specific route or a path and listening to the onCreate event and giving it a callback.

2. The onWrite function is used because we want a generic event listener to any writing operation that's present in the book event database reference. As such, the event we're going to take should have some powerful metadata, including the event type. This would mean that, based on the event, we can make different and custom behaviors. So, for instance, if we're creating a new entry, we would want to send a confirmation email. But if the event is a delete one, we would instead want to say goodbye to the user and probably convince him or her to come back.

3. We are sending emails based on the mailing service we prefer. Whether that is your open-source Nodemailer or a more powerful paid solution, the freedom is yours.

Sending re-engagement emails to inactive Firebase users

What if your users go a bit inactive, and you want to notify them about the best new thing happening within your application? In this recipe, we're going to see how we can do just that!

Getting ready

Before you start adding your function's implementation, please make sure that your project is ready for Cloud Functions.

Next, you will need to install some dependencies locally. To do this, open your function project and create a `package.json` file and copy and paste the following code snippet:

```
"dependencies": {
    "es6-promise-pool": "^2.4.4",
    "firebase-admin": "^4.1.1",
    "firebase-functions": "^0.5.1",
    "request": "^2.79.0",
    "request-promise": "^4.1.1"
}
```

How to do it...

So, if we want to perform such operations, we'll first need to figure out who the inactive users are. Then we will send an engagement email, inspired by one of the awesome samples from the Firebase team. Let's discover how we can find our inactive users and send our re-engagement email:

1. Now, let's see how we can make this happen. Please copy and paste the following code, as it will be our function declaration:

```
exports.emailNotifier =
    functions.https.onRequest((req, res) => {
```

```
getUsers().then(users => {
  // Find users that have not signed in in the
  last 1 week.
  const notifiedUsers = users.filter(
   user => parseInt(user.lastLoginAt, 10) <
    Date.now() - 7 * 24 *
 60 * 60 * 1000);
  const promisePool = new PromisePool(() => {
      if (notifiedUsers.length > 0) {
          const userToNotifiy =
           notifiedUsers.pop();
          //Get the user metadata
      admin.auth().getUser(
      userToNotifiy.localId).then(user => {
        if(user.email) {
            // TODO: Send email from here
          }
      })
      .catch(function(error) {
          console.log("[*] Error fetching user
        data:", error);
      });
    }}, MAX_CONCURRENT);
    promisePool.start().then(() => {
    res.send('[*] Successfully contacted all
      inactive users');
    });
  });
});
```

2. The next step is to implement the getUsers() function using the following code block:

```
function getUsers(userIds = [], nextPageToken,
     accessToken) {
   return
    getAccessToken(accessToken).then(accessToken =>
       {
       const options = {
         method: 'POST',
         uri:
      'https://www.googleapis.com/identitytoolkit/
             v3/relyingparty/downloadAccount?
             fields=users/localId,users/
      lastLoginAt,nextPageToken&access_token=' +
             accessToken,
             body: {
```

```
                    nextPageToken: nextPageToken,
                    maxResults: 1000
                  },
                  json: true
              };
              return rp(options).then(resp => {
                if (!resp.users) {
                  return userIds;
                }
                if </span>(resp.nextPageToken) {
                    return
            getUsers(userIds.concat(resp.users),
                    resp.nextPageToken, accessToken);
                }
                return userIds.concat</span>
                (resp.users);
              });
          });
      }
```

3. Now, let's implement the `getAccessToken()` function using the following code:

```
/**
* Returns an access token using the Google Cloud
   metadata server.
  */
function getAccessToken(accessToken) {
  // If we have an accessToken in cache to re-use we
      pass it directly.
  if (accessToken) {
      return Promise.resolve(accessToken);
  }
  const options = {
      uri:
  'http://metadata.google.internal/computeMetadata/
      v1/instance/serviceaccounts/default/token',
      headers: {'Metadata-Flavor': 'Google'},
      json: true
  };
  return rp(options).then(resp =>
    resp.access_token);
}
```

4. In case you want to upload and test your new Cloud Function, simply do the following:

   ```
   ~> firebase deploy --only functions
   ```

5. With that, your Firebase CLI will upload your function and run it on the Google server, and, as a result, will return the function URL for your needs.

Now, the service we have just described will need to run for one each week. Now, Firebase Cloud Functions doesn't currently have the ability to run cron jobs. As a result, you will need to find a suitable cron job provider and then hook it up. You can also implement and create your own cron job to suit your application's needs.

How it works...

Let's explain what just happened:

1. What we want is to find all the users within our application, that's the mission of the getUsers() function. This function will use the internal Google API to retrieve the users. The getAccessToken function is quite explicit; it will get us the access token from Google's application metadata that we can use to access the Google API servers. Over that call, we're specifying the retrieval of the users localId and lastLoginAt.

2. Within the main function call, we're filtering the users based on their lastLoginAt field to one week, and simply returning a list that suits those parameters.

3. After that, we're using the Firebase Admin SDK to find the user metadata based on their localId so we can get the user object that will eventually contain an email, which we will use to test the presence of the user. If no email was provided, which is typically the case with anonymous users, we will pass. Otherwise, we will get the email addresses and send them an email using our platform or an application mailing system of our choice.

9
We're Done, Let's Deploy

In this chapter, we're going to cover the following recipes:

- Deploying our application to Firebase
- Customizing the Firebase hosting environment

Introduction

After everything we've done, testing our application live and letting the world see how awesome it is is a must. Firebase has got us covered with an awesome static hosting service that will let us exploit something that is usually a pain in the neck, especially when we're trying to deploy our services and application, and trust me it's a pain to think about everything from security to maintainability. So, here are some of the perks you get when incorporating your application with Firebase hosting.

- Served with a secure connection, which means everything will be over HTTPS.
- Fast content delivery means that your files will be hosted/sent over CDN. This also means that users from around the world will get an even faster experience, no matter where they are.
- Rapid deployment using the Firebase CLI -we're going to see how to use it next makes the deployment process a breeze.
- One-click rollbacks mean that Firebase will keep earlier versions of your application that you've deployed, for easy and fast rolling back of errors.

All that seems great at first glance, so let's see how we can get up and running with Firebase static hosting.

Firebase hosting is exclusively for static hosting, which means that your existing backend won't be hosted - why? Well, Firebase, like we explained, is, in fact, a backend service, so now you need only care about providing the best experience ever to your users, by focusing on nothing but awesome UI/UX.

Deploying our application to Firebase

In order to get started with Firebase hosting, we need to download some dependencies first. These include the CLI itself, so let's see how we can download and install it before doing any kind of operation.

Getting ready

Head directly to your terminal of choice if you're on macOS/Linux, or cmd if you're on Windows, and type the following command:

```
~> npm install -g firebase-tools
```

In order to use npm, the node package manager, you will need to have Node.js already installed on your development machine.

How to do it...

1. Now, in the preceding command, we installed the firebase CLI utility globally on our development machine. This means that you can call it from any location within your system.
2. After installing the utility for the first time, you will be required to log in. In order to log in to your Firebase account, simply type in the following command:

```
~> firebase login
```

3. After executing it, you will get the following result:

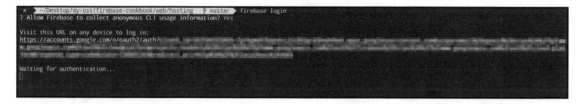

Figure 1: Logging on to our Firebase account from the CLI

4. Now, you will be redirected directly to your Google login page, where you need to pick the Google account related to your Firebase account. Once you have done that, you will receive the Google Account, Application authorization page (*Figure 2*):

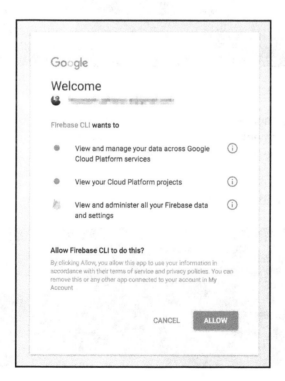

Figure 2: Google application authorization page

5. Now, click on **ALLOW** and, if everything went OK, your Firebase-CLI has been connected to your personal Firebase account.

6. After login, let's initialize our application by using the following command in your terminal of choice:

   `~> ` **`firebase init`**

7. Now you will get the following result, which will ask you to choose the type of deployment you want (*Figure 3*):

You're about to initialize a Firebase project in this directory:

 /Users/macbook/Desktop/my-oss/firebase-cookbook/web/hosting

? Which Firebase CLI features do you want to setup for this folder? Press Space to select features, then Enter to confirm your choices.
 ◯ Database: Deploy Firebase Realtime Database Rules
 ◯ Functions: Configure and deploy Cloud Functions
 ❯◯ Hosting: Configure and deploy Firebase Hosting sites

Figure 3: Choosing deployment type.

You're free to choose the type of deployment you need. In our case, we want a hosting deployment (you can choose the type of deployment using the spacebar over your keyboard and hit enter/return).

8. Then, you will need to choose the Firebase project you want to associate this deployment with (*Figure 4*):

```
? Select a default Firebase project for this directory:
  [don't setup a default project]
> firebase-cookbook (fir-cookbook)
```

Figure 4: Choosing the project we want to associate our deployment with

9. After choosing the project we want to work with, let's configure our hosting setup, following the CLI steps (*Figure 5*):

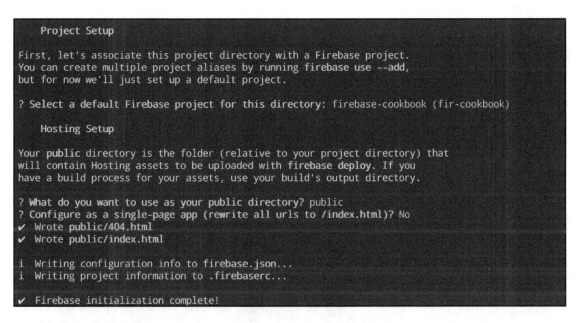

```
    Project Setup

First, let's associate this project directory with a Firebase project.
You can create multiple project aliases by running firebase use --add,
but for now we'll just set up a default project.

? Select a default Firebase project for this directory: firebase-cookbook (fir-cookbook)

    Hosting Setup

Your public directory is the folder (relative to your project directory) that
will contain Hosting assets to be uploaded with firebase deploy. If you
have a build process for your assets, use your build's output directory.

? What do you want to use as your public directory? public
? Configure as a single-page app (rewrite all urls to /index.html)? No
✔ Wrote public/404.html
✔ Wrote public/index.html

i Writing configuration info to firebase.json...
i Writing project information to .firebaserc...

✔ Firebase initialization complete!
```

Figure 5: CLI project local setup

Since I don't have anything in my project, the Firebase CLI creates a new directory called `public`, and also created some basic files such as `index.html` and `404.html` pages. Besides, the given `.html` pages will be a great starting point for your projects.

Since Firebase creates that for your outside of the box in case you just started working on your project, consider it as a best practice to start with, especially if you want to host your application later on over Firebase.

Also, a simple `firebase.json` and `.firebaserc` file that is going to host all your Firebase hosting configuration. This configuration will decide the behavior of your deployment later on and it can be customizable based on your application needs.

The `.firebaserc` file will simply hold some resource information for your project, such as your project's alias name.

10. Supposing that you already have some static content in your development machine, let's try out the deployment process. Head to your terminal of choice and write down the following command:

```
~> firebase deploy
```

After hitting *Return/Enter*, you will get the following (*Figure 6*):

```
~/Desktop/my-oss/firebase-cookbook/web/hosting    ⑂ master    firebase deploy

    Deploying to 'fir-cookbook'...

i  deploying hosting
i  hosting: preparing public directory for upload...
✔  hosting: 2 files uploaded successfully
i  starting release process (may take several minutes)...

✔  Deploy complete!

Project Console: https://console.firebase.google.com/project/fir-cookbook/overview
Hosting URL: https://fir-cookbook.firebaseapp.com
```

Figure 6: Result of successful deployment

So the preceding command will do the following:

- Uploads the contents of your `public` folder to Firebase's servers. It's the default directory name, but you can change it while doing renaming your default directory within `firebase.json` config file.
- Starts the processing and setup of your files on the server
- Returns both the `Project Console` and `Hosting URL`.

Now, copy and paste that Hosting URL over your browser in order to test it and see whether our project is up and running. I got the following result (*Figure 7*):

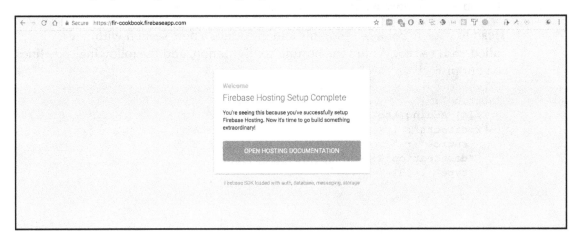

Figure 7: Our simple application hosted on Firebase Servers

How it works...

The idea behind all this CLI step checking is to have the basic configuration files in place. Also, you can configure your current development directory for future updates. The process of project configuration is done once per project, means that you will need to apply your wanted configuration each time your create/want to host your new project using Firebase.

Customizing the Firebase hosting environment

Now, since we've successfully deployed our Firebase application, it's normal to change some default values and add another value in order to get the best experience out of it. Firebase offers just that in order to have the best experience while developing and deploying your application.

How to do it...

Let us now learn how to customize Firebase using URL redirect.

Sometimes, we just want to change some URLs for some reasons, and typically sometimes we want to perform URL redirecting in order to maximise our user experience and prevent broken routes. So let's see how we can achieve that:

1. Head to your `firebase.json` file and introduce a new section within it called `redirects`. Within the hosting configuration, add the following code lines to your project:

```
"hosting": {
  //[*] Adding the redirect section
  "redirects": [ {
    "source" : "/books/firebasecookbook",
    "destination" : "/awesomebook",
    "type" : 301
  }]
}
```

Inside the `redirects` array, we're introducing the following:

- We specify the source route, in this case, `/books/firebasecookbook`
- Once we have a call over that route, we redirect the call to the `/awesomebook` route
- We specify the redirection code

Next, we will learn about customizing the Firebase hosting environment using rewrites:

- The rewrite functionality can be useful in an **SPA** (**single page application**), where we always show the main `index.html` no matter what the route is. Then, simply serve the `index.html`, which is the root and entry point of our application. Let's see how we can achieve that.
- Head again to the `firebase.json` file and write down the following code lines:

```
"hosting": {
  //[*] Adding the Rewrite section
  "rewrites": [ {
    "source": "**",
    "destination": "/index.html"
  } ]
}
```

In the preceding code, we make the following changes:

- Listen to any source we can possibly get a request from
- Serve `index.html` as a result

Last, but not least, we will customize our Firebase hosting environment with custom error pages.

Error pages are a must. They are used when your server or your application doesn't know what to do with a given request. So, as a good practice, show the error pages like the `404.html` which will be sent if Firebase can't find the wanted resource of URL.

Within Firebase, it's just enough to add those pages over your public folder or within the folder that your application is being hosted under and it will be enough to understand what it should showcase in case of an error.

How it works...

The Firebase hosting service offers much power and resilience to the deployment of the application. So by abstracting the deployment process, you will be more focused on providing the best experience you can to your clients and users. So pretty much like any HTTP service, from Nginx to Apache, route redirecting will work as expected. The hosting service will match a given route and simply redirect it to the application's predefined route, which the developer needs to set.

The only difference here is that the rules or configurations are easy to understand, and work with, means that you will spend more time improving your application functionalities rather than thinking about the application deployment different aspects. which are now managed by Firebase.

10
Integrating Firebase with NativeScript

In this chapter, we're going to cover the following recipes:

- Starting a NativeScript project
- Adding the Firebase plugin to our application
- Pushing/retrieving data from the Firebase Realtime Database
- Authenticating using anonymous or password authentication
- Authenticating using Google Sign-in
- Adding dynamic behavior using Firebase Remote Config

Introduction

Being a web developer nowadays has its very own privileges. Web developers can use their already-present superpower to create mobile applications using HTML5, CSS3, and JavaScript. That is what led major companies, such as Facebook (when they made their very own mobile application), to adopt the principle of hybrid mobile applications. But that paradigm does, in fact, have its flaws, and these flaws cause lagging. This shortcoming led companies like Telerik to think about something more native; something that uses web technologies and keeps the native performance as a requirement.

With that idea in place, NativeScript is now considered one of the hottest platforms attracting developers. By using XML, JavaScript (also Angular), minor CSS for the visual aspects, and the magical touch of incorporating native SDKs into the mix allowed the platform to adopt the best of both worlds. Plus, this allows applications to be cross-platform, which means your application is going to be able to run on Android and iOS.

In this chapter, we're going to see how we can use Firebase to create some awesome native applications.

Starting a NativeScript project

In order to start a NativeScript project, we will need to make our development environment Node.js ready. So, in order to do so, let's download Node.js. Head directly to `https://nodejs.org/en/download/` and download the most suitable version for your OS.

After you have successfully installed Node.js, you will have two utilities. One is the Node.js executable and the other will be npm or the node package manager. This will help us download our dependencies and install NativeScript locally.

How to do it...

1. In your terminal/cmd of choice, type the following command:

   ```
   ~> npm install -g nativescript
   ```

2. After installing NativeScript, you will need to add some dependencies. To know what your system is missing, simply type the following command:

   ```
   ~> tns doctor
   ```

   This command will test your system and make sure that everything is in place. If not, you'll get the missing parts.

3. In order to create a new project, you will have many options to choose from. Those options could be creating a new project with vanilla JavaScript, with Typescript, from a template, or even better, using Angular. Head directly to your working directory and type the following command:

   ```
   ~> tns create <application-name>
   ```

This command will initialize your project and install the basic needed dependencies. With that done, we're good to start working on our NativeScript project.

Adding the Firebase plugin to our application

One of NativeScript's most powerful features is the possibility of incorporating truly native SDKs. So, in this context, we can install the Firebase NativeScript on Android using the normal gradle installation command. You can also do it on iOS via a Podfile if you are running macOS and want to create an iOS application along the way. However, the NativeScript ecosystem is pluggable, which means the ecosystem has plugins that extend certain functionalities. Those plugins usually incorporate native SDKs and expose the functionalities using JavaScript so we can exploit them directly within our application.

In this recipe, we're going to use the wonderfully easy-to-use *Eddy Verbruggen* Firebase plugin, so let's see how we can add it to our project.

How to do it...

1. Head to your terminal/cmd of choice, type the following command, and hit Return/Enter respectively:

   `tns plugin add nativescript-plugin-firebase`

   This command will install the necessary plugin and do the required configuration.

2. To find out the id, open your `package.json` file where you will find the NativeScript value:

   ```
   "nativescript": {
       "id": "org.nativescript.<your-app-name>"
   }
   ```

3. Copy the id that you found in the preceding step and head over to your Firebase project console. Create a new Android/iOS application and paste that ID over your bundle name. Download the `google-service.json/GoogleServices-Info.plist` files and paste `google-server.json` in your `app/Application_Resources/Android` folder if you created an Android project. If you've created an iOS project, then paste the `GoogleServices-Info.plist` in the `app/Application_Resources/iOS` folder.

Pushing/retrieving data from the Firebase Realtime Database

Firebase stores data in a link-based manner that allows you to add and query the information really simple. The NativeScript Firebase plugin makes the operation much simpler with an easy-to-use API. So, let's discover how we can perform such operations. In this recipe, we're going to see how we can add and retrieve data in NativeScript and Firebase.

Getting ready

Before we begin, we need to make sure that our application is fully configured with Firebase. For that, you can refer to the preceding *Adding the Firebase plugin to our application* recipe, which will teach you how you can do that.

You will also need to initialize the Firebase plugin with the application. To do that, open your project, head to your app.js file, and add the following import code:

```
var firebase = require("nativescript-plugin-
    firebase");
```

This will import the Firebase NativeScript plugin. Next, add the following lines of code:

```
firebase.init({}).then((instance) => {
    console.log("[*] Firebase was successfully
        initialised");
}, (error) => {
console.log("[*] Huston we've an initialization
  error: " + error);
});
```

The preceding code will simply go and initialize Firebase within our application.

How to do it...

1. After initializing our application, let's see how we can push some data to our Firebase Realtime Database. Let's start first by adding our interface, which will look similar to the one (*Figure 1*):

Figure 1: Ideas adding page.

2. The code behind it is as follows, and you can use this to implement the addition of new data to your bucket:

```
<Page
xmlns="http://schemas.nativescript.org/tns.xsd"
navigatingTo="onNavigatingTo" class="page">
<Page.actionBar>
   <ActionBar title="Firebase CookBook"
   class="action-bar">
</ActionBar>
</Page.actionBar>
<StackLayout class="p-20">
<TextField text="{{ newIdea }}" hint="Add here your
 shiny idea"/>
 <Button text="Add new idea to my bucket" tap="{{
  addToMyBucket
 }}" </span>class</span>="btn btn-primary btn-
```

```
    active"/>
    </StackLayout>
    </Page>
```

3. Now let's see the JavaScript related to this UI for our behavior. Head to your view-model and add the following snippets inside the `createViewModel` function:

```
viewModel.addToMyBucket = () => {
    firebase.push('/ideas', {
        idea: viewModel.newIdea
    }).then((result) => {
    console.log("[*] Info : Your data was pushed !");
    }, (error) => {
  console.log("[*] Error : While pushing your data to
        Firebase, with error: " + error);
    });
}
```

If you check your Firebase database, you will find your new entry present there.

4. Once your data is live, you will need to think of a way to showcase all your shiny, new ideas. Firebase gave us a lovely event that we shall listen to whenever a new child element is created. The following code teaches you how to create the event for showcasing the addition of new child elements:

```
var onChildEvent = function(result) {
    console.log("Idea: " +
    JSON.stringify(result.value));
};
firebase.addChildEventListener(onChildEvent,
"/ideas").then((snapshot) => {
console.log("[*] Info : We've some data !");
});
```

After getting the newly-added child, it's up to you to find the proper way to bind your ideas. They are mainly going to be either lists or cards, but they could be any of the previously mentioned ones.

5. To run and experience your new feature, use the following command:

```
~> tns run android # for android
~> tns run ios # for ios
```

How it works...

Let's explain what just happened:

1. We defined a basic user interface that will serve us by adding those new ideas to our Firebase console application.
2. Next, the aim was to save all that information inside our Firebase Realtime Database using the same schema that Firebase uses. This is done via specifying a URL where all your information will be stored and then specifying the data schema. This will finally hold and define the way our data will be stored.
3. We then hooked a listener to our data URL using `firebase.addChildEventListener`. This will take a function where the next item will be held and the data URL that we want our listener hook to listen on.

4. In case you're wondering how this module or service works in NativeScript, the answer is simple. It's due to the way NativeScript works; because one of NativeScript's powerful features is the ability to use native SDKs. So in this case, we're using and implementing the Firebase Database Android/iOS SDKs for our needs, and the plugin APIs we're using are the JavaScript abstraction of how we want to exploit our native calls.

Authenticating using anonymous or password authentication

As we all know, Firebase supports both anonymous and password-based authentication, each with its own, suitable use case. So in this recipe, we're going to see how we can perform both anonymous and password authentication.

Getting ready

Before we begin, we need to make sure that our application is fully configured with Firebase. Please check the *Adding the Firebase plugin to our application* recipe from this chapter, which will teach you how you can do that.

You will also need to initialize the Firebase plugin with the application. To do that, open your project, head to your app.js file, and add the following import:

```
var firebase = require("nativescript-plugin-
   firebase");
```

This will import the Firebase NativeScript plugin. Next, add the following lines of code:

```
firebase.init({}).then((instance) => {
console.log("[*] Firebase was successfully
initialised");
}, (error) => {
console.log("[*] Huston we've an initialization
 error: " + error);
});
```

The preceding code will go and initialize Firebase within our application.

How to do it...

1. Before we start, we need to create some UI elements. Your page will look similar to this one after you finish (*Figure 2*):

Figure 2: Application login page.

2. Now open your login page and add the following code snippets there:

```
<Page
 xmlns="http://schemas.nativescript.org/tns.xsd"
navigatingTo="onNavigatingTo" class="page">
<Page.actionBar>
<ActionBar title="Firebase CookBook" icon=""
class="action-bar">
</ActionBar>
</Page.actionBar>
<StackLayout>
    <Label text="Login Page" textWrap="true"
     style="font-weight:
    bold; font-size: 18px; text-align: center;
     padding:20"/>
  <TextField hint="Email" text="{{ user_email }}" />
    <TextField hint="Password" text="{{
```

```
      user_password }}"
    secure="true"/&gt;<Button text="LOGIN" tap="{{
    passLogin }}"
      class="btn btn-primary btn-active" />
      <Button text="Anonymous login" tap="{{ anonLogin
      }}"
        class="btn btn-success"/>
  </StackLayout>
  </Page>
```

3. Save that. Let's now look at the variables and functions in our view-model file. For that, let's implement the `passLogin` and `anonLogin` functions. The first one will be our normal email and password authentication, and the second will be our anonymous login function. To make this implementation come alive, type the following code lines on your page:

```
viewModel.anonLogin = () => {
    firebase.login({
        type: firebase.LoginType.ANONYMOUS
    }).then((result) => {
        console.log("[*] Anonymous Auth Response:" +
        JSON.stringify(result));
    },(errorMessage) => {
        console.log("[*] Anonymous Auth Error:
        "+errorMessage);
    });
}

viewModel.passLogin = () => {
  let email = viewModel.user_email;
  let pass = viewModel.user_password;
  firebase.login({
      type: firebase.LoginType.PASSWORD,
      passwordOptions: {
          email: email,
          password: pass
      }
  }).then((result) => {
        console.log("[*] Email/Pass Response : " +
        JSON.stringify(result));
  }, (error) => {
    console.log("[*] Email/Pass Error : " +
    error);
  });
}
```

4. Now, simply save your file and run it using the following command:

```
~> tns run android # for android
~> tns run ios # for ios
```

How it works...

Let's quickly understand what we've just done in the recipe:

1. We've built the UI we needed as per the authentication type. If we want the email and password one, we will need the respective fields, whereas, for anonymous authentication, all we need is a button.
2. Then, for both functions, we call the Firebase login button specifying the connection type for both cases. After finishing that part, it's up to you to define what is next and to retrieve that metadata from the API for your own needs later on.

Authenticating using Google Sign-In

Google Sign-In is one of the most popular integrated services in Firebase. It does not require any extra hustle, has the most functionality, and is popular among many apps. In this recipe, we're going to see how we can integrate Firebase Google Sign-In with our NativeScript project.

Getting ready

Before we begin, we need to make sure that our application is fully configured with Firebase. For that, please check the *Adding the Firebase plugin to our application* recipe within this chapter, which will teach you how you can do just that.

You will also need to initialize the Firebase plugin within the application. To do that, open your project, head to your `app.js` file, and add the following line:

```
var firebase = require("nativescript-plugin-
firebase");
```

This will import the Firebase NativeScript plugin. Next, add the following lines of code:

```
firebase.init({}).then((instance) => {
    console.log("[*] Firebase was successfully
    initialised");
}, (error) => {
    console.log("[*] Huston we've an initialization
    error: " + error);
});
```

The preceding code will go and initialize Firebase within our application.

We will also need to install some dependencies. For that, underneath the `NativeScript-plugin-firebase` folder | **platform** | **Android** | `include.gradle` file, uncomment the following entry for Android:

```
compile "com.google.android.gms:play-services-
    auth:$googlePlayServicesVersion"
```

Now save and build your application using the following command:

```
~> tns build android
```

Or uncomment this entry if you're building an iOS application:

```
pod 'GoogleSignIn'
```

Then, build your project using the following command:

```
~> tns build ios
```

How to do it...

1. First, you will need to create your button. So for this to happen, please go to your `login-page.xml` file and add the following button declaration:

```
<Button text="Google Sign-in" tap="{{ googleLogin
}}"
 class="btn" style="color:red"/>
```

2. Now let's implement the `googleLogin()` function by using the following code snippet:

```
viewModel.googleLogin = () => {
    firebase.login({
```

```
        type: firebase.LoginType.GOOGLE,
    }).then((result) => {
      console.log("[*] Google Auth Response: " +
  JSON.</span>stringify(result));
    },(errorMessage) => {
      console.log("[*] Google Auth Error: " +
      errorMessage);
    });
  }
```

3. To build and experience your new feature, use the following command:

```
~> tns run android # for android
~> tns run ios # for ios
```

Now, once you click on the Google authentication button, you should have the following (*Figure 3*):

Figure 3: Account picking after clicking on Google Login button.

Don't forget to add your SHA-1 fingerprint code or the authentication process won't finish.

How it works...

Let's explain what just happened in the preceding code:

1. We added the new button for the Google authentication. Within the tap event of this button, we gave it the `googleLogin()` function.

2. Within `googleLogin()`, we used the Firebase login button giving it `firebase.LoginType.GOOGLE` as type. Notice that, similar to normal Google authentication on a web platform, we can also give the `hd` or the `hostedDomain` option. We could also use the option of filtering the connection hosting we want by adding the following option under the login type:

    ```
    googleOptions: { hostedDomain: "<your-host-name>" }
    ```

    The *hd* option or the *hostedDomain* is simply what's after the @ sign in an email address. So, for example, in the email ID *cookbook@packtpub.com* the hosted domain is *packtpub.com*. For some apps, you might want to limit the email ID used by users when they connect to your application to just that host. This can be done by providing only the **hostedDomain** parameter in the code line pertaining to the storage of the email address.

3. When you look at the actual way we're making these calls, you will see that it's due to the powerful NativeScript feature that lets us exploit native SDK. If you remember the *Getting ready* section of this recipe, we uncommented a section where we installed the native SDK for both Android and iOS. Besides the NativeScript firebase plugin, you can also exploit the Firebase Auth SDK, which will let you exploit all supported Firebase authentication methods.

Adding dynamic behavior using Firebase Remote Config

Remote Config is one of the hottest features of Firebase and lets us play with all the different application configurations without too much of a headache. By a headache, we mean the process of building, testing, and publishing, which usually takes a lot of our time, even if it's just to fix a small float number that might be wrong. So in this recipe, we're going to see how we can use Firebase Remote Config within our application.

Getting ready

In case you didn't choose the functionality by default when you created your application, please head to your `build.gradle` and `Podfile` and uncomment the Firebase Remote Config line in both files or in the environment you're using with your application.

How to do it...

Actually, the integration part of your application is quite easy. The tricky part is when you want to toggle states or alter some configuration. So think upon that heavily, because it will affect how your application works and will also affect the way you change properties.

1. Let's suppose that within this NativeScript application we want to have a mode called Ramadan mode. We want to create this mode for a special month where we wish to offer discounts, help our users with new promos, or even change our user interface to suit the spirit of it. So, let's see how we can do that:

```
firebase.getRemoteConfig({
    developerMode: true,
    cacheExpirationSeconds: 1,
    properties: [{
      key: "ramadan_promo_enabled",
      default: false
    }
}).then(function (result) {
    console.log("Remote Config: " +
  JSON.stringify(
result.properties.ramadan_promo_enabled));
    //TODO : Use the value to make changes.
});
```

2. In the preceding code, and because we are still in development mode, we set that we want the `developerMode` to be activated. We also set the `cacheExpirationSeconds` to be one second. This is important because we don't want our settings to take a long time until they affect our application during the development phase. This will set the **throttled mode** to true, which will make the application fetch or look for new data every second to our Firebase remote configurations.

3. We can set the default values of each and every item within our Firebase remote configuration. This value will be the starting point for fetching any new values that might be present over the Firebase project console.

4. Now, let's see how we can wire that value from the project console. To do this, head to your Firebase project **Console | Remote Config** Section | **ADD YOUR FIRST PARAMETER** Button (*Figure 4*):

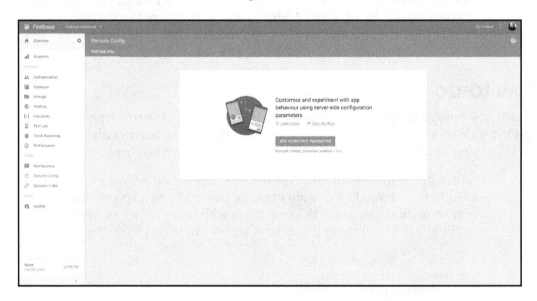

Figure 4: Firebase Remote Config Parameter adding section.

5. Next, you will get a modal where you will add your properties and their values. Make sure to add the exact same one that's in your code otherwise it won't work. The following screenshot shows the **PARAMETERS** tab of the console where you will add the properties (*Figure 5*):

Figure 5: While adding the new parameter

After adding them, click on the **PUBLISH CHANGES** button (*Figure 6*):

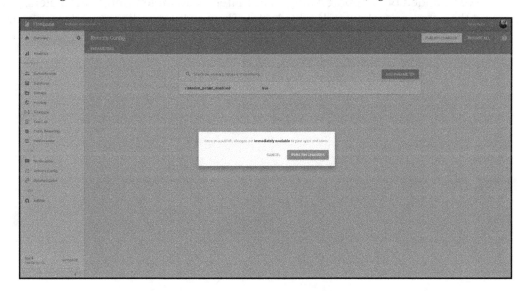

Figure 6: Publishing the new created Parameter.

With that, you're done.

7. Exit your application and open it back up again. Watch how your console and your application fetches the new values. Then, it's up to you and your application to make the needed changes once the values are changed.

How it works...

Let's explain what just happened:

1. We added back our dependencies from the `build.gradle` and Podfile so we can support the functionality we want to use.

2. We've selected and added the code that will be responsible for giving the default values and for fetching the new changes. We have also activated the **developer mode**, which will help out in our development and staging phases. This mode will be disabled once we're in production. We've set the *cache expiration time*, which is essential while being in development so we can retrieve those values in a fast way. This too will be changed in production, by giving the cache more expiration time, because we don't want to jeopardize our application with high-throttled operations every second.

3. We've added our support config in our Firebase Remote Config parameters, gave it the necessary value, and published it. This final step will control the way our application feels and looks like each new change.

11
Integrating Firebase with Android/iOS Natively

In this chapter, we're going to cover the following recipes:

- Implementing the pushing and retrieving of data from Firebase Realtime Database
- Implementing anonymous authentication
- Implementing password authentication on iOS
- Implementing password authentication on Android
- Implementing Google Sign-in authentication
- Implementing Facebook login authentication
- Generating a crash report using Firebase Crash Report
- Adding dynamic behavior using Firebase Remote Config in Android
- Adding dynamic behavior using Firebase Remote Config in iOS

Introduction

In many cases, people tend to prefer the native mobile experience on many platforms, whether it is Android or iOS. That said, many web-free present platforms have emerged that use nothing but a mobile application and Firebase. These have ended up being efficient in terms of freedom from any hustle that you might get if you had introduced your very own web platform.

In this chapter, we're going to see how we can integrate Firebase within a native context, basically over an iOS and Android application, by moving our attention from the web to the mobile-first experience. We will show you how to implement some of the basic, as well as advanced features, that you might find in any modern mobile application in both ecosystems, Android and iOS. So let's get busy!

Implementing the pushing and retrieving of data from Firebase Realtime Database

In this recipe, we're going to see how we can exploit the powerful Realtime Database on Android and iOS. We will also see how we can send and retrieve data in a real-time way.

How to do it...

We're going to start first with Android and see how we can manage this feature:

1. First, head to your Android Studio project that we created early on in Chapter 1, *Firebase - Getting Started*. Now that you have opened your project, let's move on to integrating the Realtime Database.

2. In your project, head to the Menu bar, navigate to **Tools** | **Firebase**, and then select **Realtime Database**. Now click **Save and retrieve data**. Since we've already connected our Android application to Firebase, let's now add the Firebase Realtime Database dependencies locally by clicking on the **Add the Realtime Database to your app** button. This will give you a screen that looks like the following screenshot:

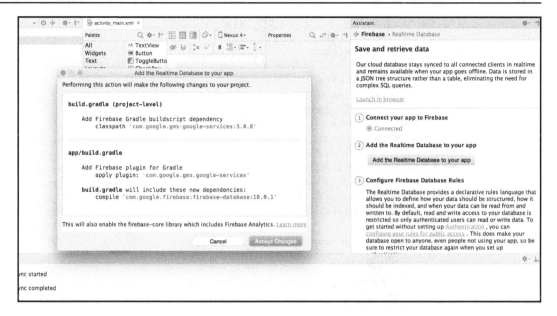

Figure 1: Android Studio Firebase integration section

3. Click on the **Accept Changes** button and the gradle will add these new dependencies to your gradle file and download and build the project.

   Now we've created this simple wish list application. It might not be the most visually pleasing but will serve us well in this experiment with `TextEdit`, a `Button`, and a `ListView`.

4. So, in our experiment we want to do the following:
   - Add a new wish to our wish list Firebase Database
   - See the wishes underneath our `ListView`

5. Let's start with adding that list of data to our Firebase. Now head to your `MainActivity.java` file of any other activity related to your project and add the following code:

```
//[*] UI reference.
EditText wishListText;
Button addToWishList;
ListView wishListview;

// [*] Getting a reference to the Database Root.
DatabaseReference fRootRef =
FirebaseDatabase.getInstance().getReference();
```

```java
//[*] Getting a reference to the wishes list.
DatabaseReference wishesRef =
  fRootRef.child("wishes");

protected void onCreate(Bundle savedInstanceState) {
    super.onCreate(savedInstanceState);
    setContentView(R.layout.activity_main);
    //[*] UI elements
    wishListText = (EditText)
findViewById(R.id.wishListText);
    addToWishList = (Button)
 findViewById(R.id.addWishBtn);
    wishListview = (ListView)
findViewById(R.id.wishsList);
}
    @Override
     protected void onStart() {
      super.onStart();
    //[*] Listening on Button click event
    addToWishList.setOnClickListener(new
     View.OnClickListener() {
      @Override
      public void onClick(View v) {
//[*] Getting the text from our EditText UI Element.
        String wish =
    wishListText.getText().toString();
    //[*] Pushing the Data to our Database.
        wishesRef.push().setValue(wish);
        AlertDialog alertDialog = new
      AlertDialog.Builder(MainActivity.this).create();
        alertDialog.setTitle("Success");
      alertDialog.setMessage("wish was added to Firebase");
        alertDialog.show();
  }
 });
 }
```

In the preceding code, we're doing the following:

- Getting a reference to our UI elements
- Since everything in Firebase starts with a reference, we're grabbing ourselves a reference to the root element in our database
- We are getting another reference to the wishes child method from the root reference
- Over the OnCreate() method, we are binding all the UI-based references to the actual UI widgets

- Over the `OnStart()` method, we're doing the following:
  - Listening to the button click event and grabbing the `EditText` content
  - Using the `wishesRef.push().setValue()` method to push the content of the `EditText` automatically to Firebase, then we are displaying a simple AlertDialog as the UI preferences

6. However, the preceding code is not going to work. This is strange since everything is well configured, but the problem here is that the Firebase Database is secured out of the box with authorization rules. Read more about this in `Chapter 5`, *Securing Application Flow with Firebase Rules*.

7. So, head to **Database** | **RULES** and change the rules there, and then publish. After that is done, the result will look similar to the following screenshot:

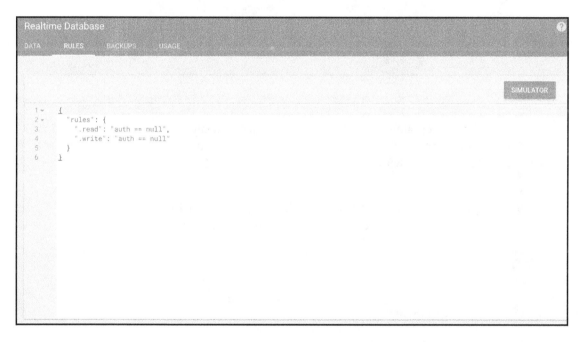

Figure 2: Firebase Realtime Database authorization section

8. After saving and launching the application, the pushed data result will look like this:

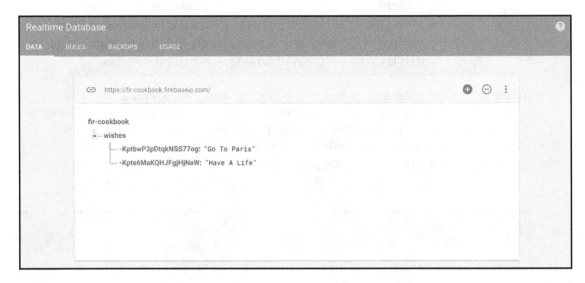

Figure 3: Firebase Realtime Database after adding a new wish to the wishes collection

 Firebase creates the child element in case you didn't create it yourself. This is great because we can create and implement any data structure we want, however, we want.

9. Next, let's see how we can retrieve the data we sent. Move back to your `onStart()` method and add the following code lines:

```
wishesRef.addChildEventListener(new
  ChildEventListener() {
    @Override
    public void onChildAdded(DataSnapshot
      dataSnapshot, String s)        {
        //[*] Grabbing the data Snapshot
        String newWish =
      dataSnapshot.getValue(String.class);
        wishes.add(newWish);
        adapter.notifyDataSetChanged();
    }
    @Override
    public void onChildChanged(DataSnapshot
      dataSnapshot, String s) {}
    @Override
```

```
    public void onChildRemoved(DataSnapshot
    dataSnapshot) {}
    @Override
    public void onChildMoved(DataSnapshot
    dataSnapshot, String s) {}
    @Override
    public void onCancelled(DatabaseError
    databaseError) {}
});
```

10. Before you implement the preceding code, go to the `onCreate()` method and add the following line underneath the UI widget reference:

```
//[*] Adding an adapter.
adapter = new ArrayAdapter<String>(this,
R.layout.support_simple_spinner_dropdown_item,
 wishes);
//[*] Wiring the Adapter
wishListview.setAdapter(adapter);
```

11. Preceding that, in the variable declaration, simply add the following declaration:

```
ArrayList<String> wishes = new ArrayList<String>();
ArrayAdapter<String> adapter;
```

So, in the preceding code, we're doing the following:

1. Adding a new `ArrayList` and an adapter for ListView changes. We're wiring everything in the `onCreate()` method.
2. Wiring an `addChildEventListener()` in the wishes Firebase reference.
3. Grabbing the data snapshot from the Firebase Realtime Database that is going to be fired whenever we add a new wish, and then wiring the list adapter to notify the `wishListview` which is going to update our Listview content automatically.

Congratulations! You've just wired and exploited the Realtime Database functionality and created your very own wishes tracker.

Now, let's see how we can create our very own iOS wishes tracker application using nothing but Swift and Firebase:

1. Head directly to and fire up Xcode, and let's open up the project that we created in `Chapter 1`, *Firebase - Getting Started*, where we integrated Firebase. Let's work on the feature.

2. Edit your `Podfile` and add the following line:

```
pod 'Firebase/Database'
```

This will download and install the Firebase Database dependencies locally, in your very own awesome wishes tracker application. There are two view controllers, one for the wishes table and the other one for adding a new wish to the wishes list, the following represents the main wishes list view.

Figure 4: iOS application wishes list view

Once we click on the + sign button in the Header, we'll be navigated with a segueway to a new ViewModal, where we have a text field where we can add our new wish and a button to push it to our list.

Figure 5: Wishes iOS application, in new wish ViewModel

3. Over `addNewWishesViewController.swift`, which is the view controller for adding the new wish view, after adding the necessary `UITextField`, `@IBOutlet` and the button `@IBAction`, replace the autogenerated content with the following code lines:

```
import UIKit
import FirebaseDatabase
class newWishViewController: UIViewController {
    @IBOutlet weak var wishText: UITextField

    //[*] Adding the Firebase Database Reference
    var ref: FIRDatabaseReference?
    override func viewDidLoad() {
       super.viewDidLoad()
       ref = FIRDatabase.database().reference()
    }
    @IBAction func addNewWish(_ sender: Any) {
    let newWish = wishText.text // [*] Getting the
    UITextField content.
    self.ref?.child("wishes").childByAutoId().setValue(
    newWish!)
    presentedViewController?.dismiss(animated: true,
    completion:nil)
    }
}
```

In the preceding code, besides the self-explanatory UI element code, we're doing the following:

- We're using the `FIRDatabaseReference` and creating a new Firebase reference, and we're initializing it with `viewDidLoad()`.
  - Within the `addNewWish` IBAction (function), we're getting the text from the `UITextField`, calling for the "wishes" child, then we're calling `childByAutoId()`, which will create an automatic id for our data (consider it a push function, if you're coming from JavaScript). We're simply setting the value to whatever we're going to get from the TextField.
- Finally, we're dismissing the current ViewController and going back to the `TableViewController` which holds all our wishes.

Implementing anonymous authentication

Authentication is one of the most tricky, time-consuming and tedious tasks in any web application. and of course, maintaining the best practices while doing so is truly a hard job to maintain. For mobiles, it's even more complex, because if you're using any traditional application it will mean that you're going to create a REST endpoint, an endpoint that will take an email and password and return either a session or a token, or directly a user's profile information. In Firebase, things are a bit different and in this recipe, we're going to see how we can use anonymous authentication—we will explain that in a second.

You might wonder, but why? The why is quite simple: to give users an anonymous temporal, to protect data and to give users an extra taste of your application's inner soul. So let's see how we can make that happen.

How to do it...

We will first see how we can implement anonymous authentication in Android:

1. Fire up your Android Studio. Before doing anything, we need to get some dependencies first, speaking, of course, of the Firebase Auth library that can be downloaded by adding this line to the `build.gradle` file under the dependencies section:

    ```
    compile 'com.google.firebase:firebase-auth:11.0.2'
    ```

2. Now simply **Sync** and you will be good to start adding Firebase Authentication logic. Let us see what we're going to get as a final result:

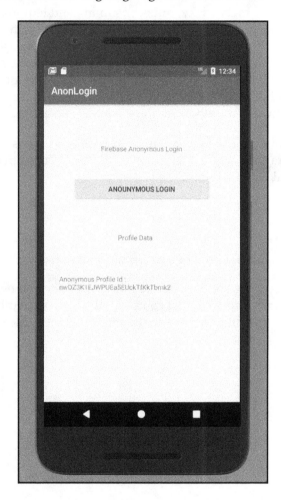

Figure 6: Android application: anonymous login application

A simple UI with a button and a TextView, where we put our user data after a successful authentication process.

Here's the code for that simple UI:

```xml
<?xml version="1.0" encoding="utf-8"?>
<android.support.constraint.ConstraintLayout
  xmlns:android="http://schemas.android.com/
    apk/res/android"
xmlns:app="http://schemas.android.com/apk/res-auto"
xmlns:tools="http://schemas.android.com/tools"
android:layout_width="match_parent"
android:layout_height="match_parent"
tools:context="com.hcodex.anonlogin.MainActivity">

    <Button
      android:id="@+id/anonLoginBtn"
      android:layout_width="289dp"
      android:layout_height="50dp"
      android:text="Anonumous Login"
      android:layout_marginRight="8dp"
      app:layout_constraintRight_toRightOf="parent"
      android:layout_marginLeft="8dp"
      app:layout_constraintLeft_toLeftOf="parent"
      android:layout_marginTop="47dp"
      android:onClick="anonLoginBtn"
        app:layout_constraintTop_toBottomOf=
          "@+id/textView2"
      app:layout_constraintHorizontal_bias="0.506"
      android:layout_marginStart="8dp"
      android:layout_marginEnd="8dp" />

  <TextView
    android:id="@+id/textView2"
    android:layout_width="wrap_content"
    android:layout_height="wrap_content"
    android:text="Firebase Anonymous Login"
    android:layout_marginLeft="8dp"
    app:layout_constraintLeft_toLeftOf="parent"
    android:layout_marginRight="8dp"
    app:layout_constraintRight_toRightOf="parent"
    app:layout_constraintTop_toTopOf="parent"
    android:layout_marginTop="80dp" />

  <TextView
    android:id="@+id/textView3"
    android:layout_width="wrap_content"
    android:layout_height="wrap_content"
    android:text="Profile Data"
    android:layout_marginTop="64dp"
    app:layout_constraintTop_toBottomOf=
```

```xml
            "@+id/anonLoginBtn"
            android:layout_marginLeft="156dp"
            app:layout_constraintLeft_toLeftOf="parent" />

    <TextView
            android:id="@+id/profileData"
            android:layout_width="349dp"
            android:layout_height="175dp"
            android:layout_marginBottom="28dp"
            android:layout_marginEnd="8dp"
            android:layout_marginLeft="8dp"
            android:layout_marginRight="8dp"
            android:layout_marginStart="8dp"
            android:layout_marginTop="8dp"
            android:text=""
            app:layout_constraintBottom_toBottomOf="parent"
            app:layout_constraintHorizontal_bias="0.526"
            app:layout_constraintLeft_toLeftOf="parent"
            app:layout_constraintRight_toRightOf="parent"
            app:layout_constraintTop_toBottomOf=
            "@+id/textView3" />
    </android.support.constraint.ConstraintLayout>
```

3. Now, let's see how we can wire up our Java code:

```java
//[*] Step 1 : Defining Logic variables.
FirebaseAuth anonAuth;
FirebaseAuth.AuthStateListener authStateListener;
@Override
protected void onCreate(Bundle savedInstanceState) {
    super.onCreate(savedInstanceState);
    anonAuth = FirebaseAuth.getInstance();
    setContentView(R.layout.activity_main);
};


//[*] Step 2: Listening on the
  Login button click event.
  public void anonLoginBtn(View view) {
    anonAuth.signInAnonymously()
    .addOnCompleteListener(
    this, new OnCompleteListener<AuthResult>() {
    @Override public void onComplete(@NonNull
    Task<AuthResult> task) {
      if(!task.isSuccessful()) {
        updateUI(null);
          } else {
          FirebaseUser fUser =
```

```
            anonAuth.getCurrentUser();
            Log.d("FIRE", fUser.getUid());
            updateUI(fUser);
                }
        });
    }
    }
//[*] Step 3 : Getting UI Reference
private void updateUI(FirebaseUser user) {
profileData = (TextView) findViewById(
 R.id.profileData);
 profileData.append("Anonymous Profile Id : \n" +
 user.getUid());
 }
```

Now, let's see how we can implement anonymous authentication on iOS:

What we'll achieve in this test is the following :

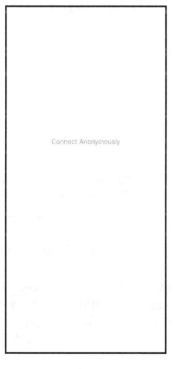

Connect Anonymously

Figure 7: iOS application, anonymous login application

1. Before doing anything, we need to download and install the Firebase authentication dependency first. Head directly over to your `Podfile` and the following line:

```
pod 'Firebase/Auth'
```

2. Then simply save the file, and on your terminal, type the following command:

```
~> pod install
```

This will download the needed dependency and configure our application accordingly.

3. Now create a simple UI with a button and after configuring your UI button `IBAction` reference, let's add the following code:

```
@IBAction func connectAnon(_ sender: Any) {
Auth.auth().signInAnonymously() { (user, error) in
 if let anon = user?.isAnonymous {
 print("i'm connected anonymously here's my id \
  (user?.uid)")
 }
}
}
```

How it works...

Let's digest the preceding code:

1. We're defining some basic logic variables; we're taking basically a TextView, where we'll append our results and define the Firebase `anonAuth` variable. It's of `FirebaseAuth` type, which is the starting point for any authentication strategy that we might use.
2. Over `onCreate`, we're initializing our Firebase reference and fixing our content view.
3. We're going to authenticate our user by clicking a button bound with the `anonLoginBtn()` method. Within it, we're simply calling for the `signInAnonymously()` method, then if incomplete, we're testing if the authentication task is successful or not, else we're updating our TextEdit with the user information.
4. We're using the `updateUI` method to simply update our TextField.

Pretty simple steps. Now simply build and run your project and test your shiny new features.

Implementing password authentication on iOS

Email and password authentication is the most common way to authenticate anyone and it can be a major risk point if done wrong. Using Firebase will remove that risk and make you think of nothing but the UX that you will eventually provide to your users. In this recipe, we're going to see how you can do this on iOS.

How to do it...

1. Let's suppose you've created your awesome UI with all text fields and buttons and wired up the email and password `IBOutlets` and the `IBAction` login button. Let's see the code behind the awesome, quite simple password authentication process:

```
import UIKit
import Firebase
import FirebaseAuth
class EmailLoginViewController: UIViewController {
    @IBOutlet weak var emailField: UITextField!
    @IBOutlet weak var passwordField: UITextField!
    override func viewDidLoad() {
      super.viewDidLoad()
    }
    @IBAction func loginEmail(_ sender: Any) {
      if self.emailField.text</span> == "" ||
      self.passwordField.text == "" {
      //[*] Prompt an Error
      let alertController = UIAlertController(title:
      "Error", message: "Please enter an email
      and password.", preferredStyle: .alert)
      let defaultAction = UIAlertAction(title: "OK",
      style: .cancel, handler: nil)
      alertController.addAction(defaultAction)
      self.present(alertController, animated: true,
        completion: nil)
    } else {
      FIRAuth.auth()?.signIn(withEmail:
```

```
    self.emailField.text!, password:
    self.passwordField.text!) { (user, error) in
       if error == nil {
          //[*] TODO: Navigate to Application Home Page.
       } else {
          //[*] Alert in case we've an error.
          let alertController = UIAlertController(title:
          "Error", message: error?.localizedDescription,
          preferredStyle: .alert)
          let defaultAction = UIAlertAction(title: "OK",
          style: .cancel, handler: nil)
           alertController.addAction(defaultAction)
           self.present(alertController, animated: true,
          completion: nil)
           }
       }
     }
   }
 }
```

How it works ...

Let's digest the preceding code:

1. We're simply adding some IBOutlets and adding the IBAction login button.
2. Over the loginEmail function, we're doing two things:
    1. If the user didn't provide any email/password, we're going to prompt them with an error alert indicating the necessity of having both fields.
    2. We're simply calling for the FIRAuth.auth().singIn() function, which in this case takes an *Email* and a *Password.* Then we're testing if we have any errors. Then, and only then, we might navigate to the app home screen or do anything else we want. We prompt them again with the Authentication Error message.

And as simple as that, we're done. The User object will be transported, as well, so you may do any additional processing to the name, email, and much more.

Implementing password authentication on Android

To make things easier in terms of Android, we're going to use the awesome Firebase Auth UI. Using the Firebase Auth UI will save a lot of hassle when it comes to building the actual user interface and handling the different intent calls between the application activities. Let's see how we can integrate and use it for our needs.

Getting ready

Let's start first by configuring our project and downloading all the necessary dependencies. Head to your `build.gradle` file and copy/paste the following entry:

```
compile 'com.firebaseui:firebase-ui-auth:3.0.0'
```

Now, simply sync and you will be good to start.

How to do it...

Now, let's see how we can make the functionality work:

1. Declare the FirebaseAuth reference, plus add another variable that we will need later on:

```
FirebaseAuth auth;
private static final int RC_SIGN_IN = 17;
```

2. Now, inside your `onCreate` method, add the following code:

```
auth = FirebaseAuth.getInstance();
 if(auth.getCurrentUser() != null) {
    Log.d("Auth", "Logged in successfully");
} else {
    startActivityForResult(
      AuthUI.getInstance()
        .createSignInIntentBuilder()
        .setAvailableProviders(
        Arrays.asList(new
        AuthUI.IdpConfig.Builder(
  AuthUI.EMAIL_PROVIDER).build())).build(),
  RC_SIGN_IN);findViewById(R.id.logoutBtn)
  .setOnClickListener(this);
```

3. Now, in your activity, implement the `View.OnClick` listener. So your class will look like the following:

```
public class MainActivity extends AppCompatActivity
implements View.OnClickListener {}
```

4. After that, implement the `onClick` function as shown here:

```
@Override
public void onClick(View v) {
   if(v.getId() == R.id.logoutBtn) {
AuthUI.getInstance().signOut(this)
.addOnCompleteListener(
new OnCompleteListener<Void>() {
 @Override
 public void onComplete(@NonNull Task<Void> task)
    {
      Log.d("Auth", "Logged out successfully");
      // TODO: make custom operation.
    }
   });
 }
}
```

5. At the end, implement the `onActivityResult` method as shown in the following code block:

```
@Override
 protected void onActivityResult(int requestCode,
  int resultCode, Intent data) {
    super.onActivityResult(requestCode,
    resultCode, data);
   if(requestCode == RC_SIGN_IN) {
     if(resultCode == RESULT_OK) {
        //User is in !
   Log.d("Auth",auth.getCurrentUser().getEmail());
        } else {
        //User is not authenticated
         Log.d("Auth", "Not Authenticated");
      }
    }
  }
```

6. Now build and run your project. You will have a similar interface to that shown in the following screenshot:

Figure 8: Android authentication using email/password: email picker

This interface will be shown in case you're not authenticated and your application will list all the saved accounts on your device. If you click on the **NONE OF THE ABOVE** button, you will be prompted with the following interface:

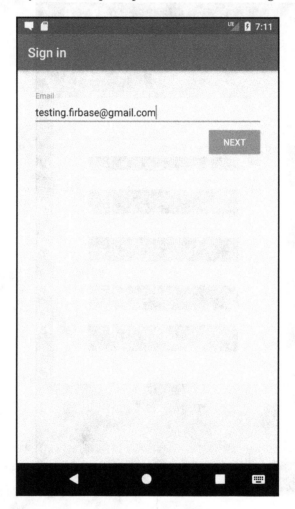

Figure 9: Android authentication email/password: adding new email

7. When you add your email and click on the **NEXT** button, the API will go and look for that user with that email in your application's users. If such an email is present, you will be authenticated, but if it's not the case, you will be redirected to the **Sign-up** activity as shown in the following screenshot:

Figure 10: Android authentication: creating a new account, with email/password/name

8. Next, you will add your name and password. And with that, you will create a new account and you will be authenticated.

How it works...

From the preceding code, it's clear that we didn't create any user interface. The Firebase UI is so powerful, so let's explore what happens:

1. The `setAvailableProviders` method will take a list of providers—those providers will be different based on your needs, so it can be any email provider, Google, Facebook, and each and every provider that Firebase supports. The main difference is that each and every provider will have each separate configuration and necessary dependencies that you will need to support the functionality.

2. Also, if you've noticed, we're setting up a logout button. We created this button mainly to log out our users and added a click listener to it. The idea here is that when you click on it, the application performs the Sign-out operation. Then you add your custom intent that will vary from a redirect to closing the application.

3. If you noticed, we're implementing the `onActivityResult` special function and this one will be our main listening point whenever we connect or disconnect from the application. Within it, we can perform different operations from resurrection to displaying toasts, to anything that you can think of.

Implementing Google Sign-in authentication

Google authentication is the process of logging in/creating an account using nothing but your existing Google account. It's easy, fast, and intuitive and removes a lot of hustle we face, usually when we register any web/mobile application. I'm talking basically about form filling. Using Firebase Google Sign-in authentication, we can manage such functionality; plus we have had the user basic metadata such as the display name, picture URL, and more. In this recipe, we're going to see how we can implement Google Sign-in functionality for both Android and iOS.

Getting ready...

Before doing any coding, it's important to do some basic configuration in our Firebase Project console.

Head directly to your Firebase project **Console** | **Authentication** | **SIGN-IN METHOD** | **Google** and simply activate the switch and follow the instructions there in order to get the client. Please notice that Google Sign-in is automatically configured for iOS, but for Android, we will need to do some custom configuration.

Let us first look at getting ready for Android to implement Google Sign-in authentication:

1. Before we start implementing the authentication functionality, we will need to install some dependencies first, so please head to your `build.gradle` file and paste the following, and then sync your build:

```
compile 'com.google.firebase:firebase-auth:11.4.2'
compile 'com.google.android.gms:play-services-
    auth:11.4.2'
```

 The dependency versions are dependable, and that means that whenever you want to install them, you will have to provide the same version for both dependencies.

Moving on to getting ready in iOS for implementation of Google Sign-in authentication:

1. In iOS, we will need to install a couple of dependencies, so please go and edit your `Podfile` and add the following lines underneath your already present dependencies, if you have any:

```
pod 'Firebase/Auth'
pod 'GoogleSignIn'
```

 In case you're wondering how to configure your iOS project with Firebase, please check `Chapter 1`, *Firebase - Getting Started*, where we configured our iOS project with Cocoapods as the dependency manager.

2. Now, in your terminal, type the following command:

```
~> pod install
```

This command will install the required dependencies and configure your project accordingly.

How to do it...

First, let us take a look at how we will implement this recipe in Android:

1. Now, after installing our dependencies, we will need to create the UI for our calls. To do that, simply copy and paste the following special button XML code into your layout:

```
<com.google.android.gms.common.SignInButton
  android:id="@+id/gbtn"
  android:layout_width="368dp"
  android:layout_height="wrap_content"
android:layout_marginLeft="16dp"
android:layout_marginTop="30dp"
app:layout_constraintLeft_toLeftOf="parent"
app:layout_constraintTop_toTopOf="parent"
android:layout_marginRight="16dp"
app:layout_constraintRight_toRightOf="parent" />
```

The result will be this:

Figure 11: Google Sign-in button after the declaration

2. After doing that, let's see the code behind it:

```
SignInButton gBtn;
FirebaseAuth mAuth;
GoogleApiClient mGoogleApiClient;
private final static int RC_SIGN_IN = 3;
FirebaseAuth.AuthStateListener mAuthListener;

 @Override
  protected void onStart() {
  super.onStart();

  mAuth.addAuthStateListener(mAuthListener);
  }
 @Override
 protected void onCreate(Bundle savedInstanceState) {
  super.onCreate(savedInstanceState);
  setContentView(R.layout.activity_main);
   mAuth = FirebaseAuth.getInstance();
   gBtn = (SignInButton) findViewById(R.id.gbtn);

  button.setOnClickListener(new View.OnClickListener()
    {
     @Override
     public void onClick(View v) {
         signIn();
      }
  });
  mAuthListener = new FirebaseAuth.AuthStateListener()
    {
     @Override
     public void onAuthStateChanged(@NonNull
       FirebaseAuth firebaseAuth) {
         if(firebaseAuth.getCurrentUser() != null) {
          AlertDialog alertDialog = new
        AlertDialog.Builder(MainActivity.this).create();
         alertDialog.setTitle("User");
        alertDialog.setMessage("I have a user loged
          in");
         alertDialog.show();
         }
      }
  };

  mGoogleApiClient = new GoogleApiClient.Builder(this)
    .enableAutoManage(this, new
   GoogleApiClient.OnConnectionFailedListener() {
         @Override
```

```
         public void onConnectionFailed(@NonNull
         ConnectionResult connectionResult) {
         Toast.makeText(MainActivity.this, "Something
         went wrong", Toast.LENGTH_SHORT).show();
             }
         })
         .addApi(Auth.GOOGLE_SIGN_IN_API, gso)
         .build();
         }

     GoogleSignInOptions gso = new
     GoogleSignInOptions.Builder(
     GoogleSignInOptions.DEFAULT_SIGN_IN)
     .requestEmail()
     .build();

     private void signIn() {
        Intent signInIntent =
     Auth.GoogleSignInApi.getSignInIntent(
     mGoogleApiClient);
   startActivityForResult(signInIntent, RC_SIGN_IN);
   }

   @Override
    public void onActivityResult(int requestCode, int
    resultCode, Intent data) {
    super.onActivityResult(requestCode,
     resultCode, data);
   if (requestCode == RC_SIGN_IN) {
    GoogleSignInResult result = Auth.GoogleSignInApi
     .getSignInResultFromIntent(data);
      if (result.isSuccess()) {
        // Google Sign In was successful,
          authenticate with Firebase
        GoogleSignInAccount account =
         result.getSignInAccount();
        firebaseAuthWithGoogle(account);
         } else {
       Toast.makeText(MainActivity.this,
       "Connection Error", Toast.LENGTH_SHORT).show();
       }
     }
   }

   private void firebaseAuthWithGoogle(
   GoogleSignInAccount account) {
   AuthCredential credential =
   GoogleAuthProvider.getCredential(
```

```
account.getIdToken(), null);
 mAuth.signInWithCredential(credential)
     .addOnCompleteListener(this, new
  OnCompleteListener<AuthResult>() {
        @Override
        public void onComplete(@NonNull
       Task<AuthResult> task) {
         if (task.isSuccessful()) {
           // Sign in success, update UI with the
             signed-in user's information
             Log.d("TAG",
      "signInWithCredential:success");
             FirebaseUser user =
             mAuth.getCurrentUser();
             Log.d("TAG", user.getDisplayName());
             } else {
              Log.w("TAG",
     "signInWithCredential:failure",
      task.getException());
      Toast.makeText(MainActivity.this,
    "Authentication failed.", Toast.LENGTH_SHORT)
    .show();
             }
             // ...
         }
    });
 }
```

3. Then, simply build and launch your application, click on the authentication button, and you will be greeted with the following screen:

Figure 12: Account picker, after clicking on Google Sign-in button.

4. Next, simply pick the account you want to connect with, and then you will be greeted with an alert, finishing the authentication process.

Now we will take a look at an implementation of our recipe in iOS:

1. Before we do anything, let's import the Google Sign-in as follows:

```
import GoogleSignIn
```

2. After that, let's add our Google Sign-in button; to do so, go to your Login Page ViewController and add the following line of code:

```
//Google sign in
let googleBtn = GIDSignInButton()
googleBtn.frame =CGRect(x: 16, y: 50, width:
 view.frame.width - 32, height: 50)
 view.addSubview(googleBtn)
```

```
GIDSignIn.sharedInstance().uiDelegate = self
```

The frame positioning is for my own needs—you can use it or modify the dimension to suit your application needs.

3. Now, after adding the lines above, we will get an error. This is due to our ViewController not working well with the `GIDSignInUIDelegate`, so in order to make our xCode happier, let's add it to our ViewModal declaration so it looks like the following:

```
class ViewController: UIViewController,
FBSDKLoginButtonDelegate, GIDSignInUIDelegate {}
```

Now, if you build and run your project, you will get the following:

Figure 13: iOS application after configuring the Google Sign-in button

4. Now, if you click on the **Sign in** button, you will get an exception. The reason for that is that the **Sign in** button is asking for the clientID, so to fix that, go to your `AppDelegate` file and complete the following import:

```
import GoogleSignIn
```

5. Next, add the following line of code within the application: `didFinishLaunchingWithOptions` as shown below:

```
GIDSignIn.sharedInstance().clientID =
FirebaseApp.app()?.options.clientID
```

6. If you build and run the application now, then click on the **Sign in** button, nothing will happen. Why? Because iOS doesn't know how and where to navigate to next. So now, in order to fix that issue, go to your `GoogleService-Info.plist` file, copy the value of the **REVERSED_CLIENT_ID**, then go to your project configuration. Inside the **Info** section, scroll down to the URL types, add a new URL type, and paste the link inside the **URL Schemes** field:

Figure 14: Xcode Firebase URL schema adding, to finish the Google Sign-in behavior

7. Next, within the application: open URL options, add the following line:

```
GIDSignIn.sharedInstance().handle(url,
sourceApplication:options[
UIApplicationOpenURLOptionsKey.sourceApplication] as?
String, annotation:
 options[UIApplicationOpenURLOptionsKey.annotation])
```

This will simply help the transition to the URL we already specified within the URL schemes.

8. Next, if you build and run your application, tap on the **Sign in** button and you will be redirected using the `SafariWebViewController` to the Google Sign-in page, as shown in the following screenshot:

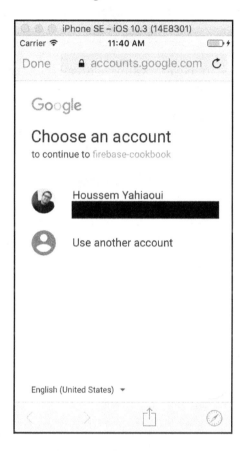

Figure 15: iOS Google account picker after clicking on Sign-in button

With that, the ongoing authentication process is done, but what will happen when you select your account and authorize the application? Typically, you need to go back to your application with all the needed profile information, don't you? isn't? Well, for now, it's not the case, so let's fix that.

9. Go back to the `AppDelegate` file and do the following:

- Add the `GIDSignInDelegate` to the app delegate declaration
- Add the following line to the application: `didFinishLaunchingWithOptions:`

```
GIDSignIn.sharedInstance().delegate = self
```

This will simply let us go back to the application with all the tokens we need to finish the authentication process with Firebase.

10. Next, we need to implement the `signIn` function that belongs to the `GIDSignInDelegate`; this function will be called once we're successfully authenticated:

```
func sign(_ signIn: GIDSignIn!, didSignInFor user:
GIDGoogleUser!, withError error: Error!) {
  if let err = error {
    print("Can't connect to Google")
    return
  }
  print("we're using google sign in", user)
}
```

Now, once you're fully authenticated, you will receive the success message over your terminal.

11. Now we can simply integrate our Firebase authentication logic. Complete the following import:

```
import FirebaseAuth
```

12. Next, inside the same `signIn` function, add the following:

```
guard let authentication = user.authentication else
  {
  return }
let credential =
  GoogleAuthProvider.credential(withIDToken:
authentication.idToken, accessToken:
  authentication.accessToken)

  Auth.auth().signIn(with: credential, completion:
  {(user, error) in
    if let error = error {
    print("[*] Can't connect to firebase, with error
      :", error)          }
```

```
    print("we have a user", user?.displayName)
    })
```

This code will use the successfully logged in user token and call the Firebase Authentication logic to create a new Firebase user. Now we can retrieve the basic profile information that Firebase delivers.

How it works...

Let's explain what we did in the Android section:

1. We activated authentication using our Google account from the Firebase project console.
2. We also installed the required dependencies, from Firebase Auth to Google services.
3. After finishing the setup, we gained the ability to create that awesome Google Sign-in special button, and we also gave it an ID for easy access.
4. We created references from `SignInButton` and `FirebaseAuth`.

Let's now explain what we just did in the iOS section:

1. We used the `GIDSignButton` in order to create the branded Google Sign-in button, and we added it to our ViewController.
2. Inside the `AppDelegate`, we made a couple of configurations so we could retrieve our `ClientID` that the button needed to connect to our application.
3. For our button to work, we used the information stored in `GoogleService-Info.plist` and created an app link within our application so we could navigate to our connection page.
4. Once everything was set, we were introduced to our application authorization page where we authorized the application and chose the account we wanted to use to connect.
5. In order to get back all the required tokens and account information, we needed to go back to the `AppDelegate` file and implement the `GIDSignInDelegate`. Within it, we could can all the account-related tokens and information, once we were successful authenticated.
6. Within the implemented `SignIn` function, we injected our regular Firebase authentication `signIn` method with all necessary tokens and information. When we built and ran the application again and signed in, we found the account used to authenticate, present in the Firebase authenticated account.

Implementing Facebook login authentication

With more than one billion users, Facebook holds basically all the connected users around the world, meaning that having a Facebook account nowadays has become a normal thing. That also means that we can authenticate people using their Facebook account to both login and create new accounts with any web/mobile application that implements Firebase Facebook login authentication. In this recipe we're going to see how we can integrate Firebase Facebook authentication with both Android and iOS, so let's get busy!

Getting ready...

Before writing any lines of code, we need to configure our Firebase application and activate the Facebook authentication. To do so, go directly to Firebase project **Console** | **Authentication** section | **SIGN-IN METHOD** | **Facebook** and simply hit the button to activate it.

You will need to create a Facebook application from the Facebook developers, platform, then you will need to copy/paste the **App ID** and **App secret** right from your Facebook application dashboard into your Firebase Facebook authentication fields.

Facebook authentication in Android

In case you created an Android application before, you might already have heard or know about the Facebook authentication, but in this recipe, we're going to cover how we can integrate Facebook OAuth using the Firebase UI Auth library.

Getting ready...

Before we start coding our application, let's install some dependencies. Go to your `build.gradle` file and paste in the following entry:

```
compile 'com.firebaseui:firebase-ui-auth:3.0.0'
compile 'com.facebook.android:facebook-login:4.27.0'
```

Now simply save and sync your project; what will happen next is that Android Studio will download and configure your project accordingly with the new dependency.

How to do it...

To save you the hassle of creating the connection button and wiring the button and metadata, Firebase offers the powerful Firebase UI for Android, where it will help us create the basic UI and wire up everything for us out of the box. So let's see how we can make it happen.

1. In your login activity, add the following variable declarations:

```
private static final int RC_SIGN_IN = 17;
FirebaseAuth auth;
```

2. Next, in your onCreate() method, add the following :

```
auth = FirebaseAuth.getInstance();
if(auth.getCurrentUser() != null) {
Log.d("Auth", "Logged in successfully");
} else {
 startActivityForResult(
        AuthUI.getInstance()
                .createSignInIntentBuilder()
                .setAvailableProviders(
                  Arrays.asList(
                        new
   AuthUI.IdpConfig.Builder(AuthUI.FACEBOOK_PROVIDER)
        .build())))
        .build(),
        RC_SIGN_IN);
 }
```

3. Now let's implement the onActivityResult() method:

```
@Override
protected void onActivityResult(int requestCode, int
resultCode, Intent data) {
super.onActivityResult(requestCode, resultCode,
  data);
if(requestCode == RC_SIGN_IN) {
   if(resultCode == RESULT_OK) {
      //User is in !
      Log.d("Auth",
  auth.getCurrentUser().getEmail());
```

```
    } else {
       //User is not authenticated
       Log.d("Auth", "Not Authenticated");
     }
   }


 }
```

4. Now, in your `value/strings.xml` file, add the following strings:

```
<string name="facebook_app_id"><your-app-id></string>
<string name="fb_login_protocol_scheme">fb<your-app-
 id>
</string>
```

5. Now, grab the app-id value from the Facebook Developer Console application project and replace those placeholders.

6. Also, inside your `AndroidManifest.xml` file, add the following :

```
<meta-data
   android:name="com.facebook.sdk.ApplicationId"
   android:value="@string/facebook_app_id"/>
 <activity
   android:name="com.facebook.FacebookActivity"
   android:configChanges=
  "keyboard|keyboardHidden|screenLayout|screenSize|
   orientation" android:label="@string/app_name" />

   <activity
android:name="com.facebook.CustomTabActivity"
android:exported="true">
<intent-filter>
 <action android:name="android.intent.action.VIEW" />
   <category
     android:name="android.intent.category.DEFAULT" />
   <category
    android:name="android.intent.category.BROWSABLE" />
     <data
    android:scheme="@string/fb_login_protocol_scheme" />
  </intent-filter>
</activity>
```

Those intents and activities will help later on within the authentication process.

7. Now, simply build and run your project and you will have the following login layout:

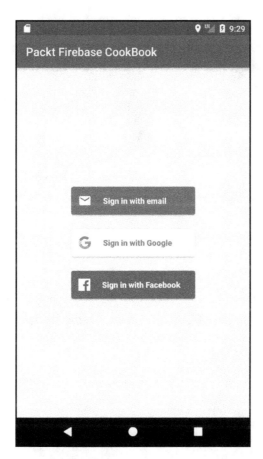

Figure 16: After adding the Facebook Sign-in button using Firebase UI

The preceding image, (*Figure 16*) is the Firebase
UI `setAvailableProviders()` result. The other email/Sign-in with Google options are present in case you want to support them as well.

8. Now, if you click on the **Sign in with Facebook** button, you will be redirected to the following Facebook connection page (*Figure 17*).

Figure 17: Facebook account connection after clicking on login button with no account presence

Once you add your credentials, you will be redirected once again to the authorization page (*Figure 18*).

Figure 18: Facebook account, Facebook application authorization

Once you click on the continue button, `onActivityResult()` will be called, and if everything is all right, your Facebook email address will be shown in the console, and with that, you're done.

How it works

Let's explain what just happened:

1. We used the Firebase UI so we could have an easy and simple UI out of the box, so we didn't do any UI management from our side. The SDK built everything for us using nothing but an API call inside the `setAvailableProviders()` method as presented in the preceding section.

2. We implemented the `onActivityResult()` method to retrieve the basic profile information in case everything went all right. This function was where we pulled all our post-authentication logic, from redirection to information and profile storing.

Facebook authentication in iOS

Facebook authentication is an already present topic, but within the scope of this recipe, we're going to cover how we can add the Firebase side by side with the Facebook authentication logic.

Getting ready

Before we actually start implementing the functionalities, please go and edit your `Podfile` and paste in the following entry:

```
pod 'FBSDKCoreKit'
pod 'FBSDKLoginKit'
pod 'Firebase/Auth'
```

Now save, and then in your favorite terminal of choice, type the following command:

```
~> pod install
```

This command will download the needed dependency and its dependencies, and configure your project accordingly. After that, in your project finder, open the .xcworkspace version of your project; it's the version that comes bundled with the new dependencies and changes.

Now, open your project with `info.plist` as the source code, and add the following lines just before last `</dict>` markup closing:

```
<key>CFBundleURLTypes</key>
 <array>
   <dict>
   <key>CFBundleURLSchemes</key>
   <array>
       <string>fbyour-facebook-app-id</string>
       </array>
     </dict>
 </array>
 <key>FacebookAppID</key>
 <string>your-facebook-app-id</string>
 <key>FacebookDisplayName</key>
 <string>your-facbook-app-name-from-facebook-
   developer-  site</string>
   <key>LSApplicationQueriesSchemes</key>
 <array>
     <string>fbapi</string>
     <string>fb-messenger-api</string>
     <string>fbauth2</string>
     <string>fbshareextension</string>
 </array>
```

Regarding the `FacebookDisplayName` and `FacebookAppID` string values, you can retrieve them from the Firebase developer console.

How to do it...

In your `AppDelegate` file, add the following imports:

```
import Firebase
import FBSDKCoreKit
```

Next, underneath your `didFinishLaunchingWithOptions`, add the following lines:

```
FirebaseApp.configure()
FBSDKApplicationDelegate.sharedInstance().
application(application,
didFinishLaunchingWithOptions: launchOptions)
```

The first line will initialize the usage of Firebase within our application and will make sure that we're exploiting the Facebook capabilities and also initiating it with the startup of our application.

Next, within the same file add the following:

```
func application(_ app: UIApplication, open url: URL,
options: [UIApplicationOpenURLOptionsKey : Any] =
  [:]) -> Bool {
  let handled =
FBSDKApplicationDelegate.sharedInstance()
.application(app, open: url, sourceApplication:
 options [UIApplicationOpenURLOptionsKey
 .sourceApplication] as! String, annotation:
  options[UIApplicationOpenURLOptionsKey
  .annotation])
   return handled
}
```

We will explain why we've added that function later on.

Now, inside your `ViewController`, add the following imports as well:

```
import FBSDKLoginKit
import FirebaseAuth
```

Now, inside `viewDidLoad()`, add the following :

```
let loginButton = FBSDKLoginButton()
 loginButton.frame = CGRect(x: 16, y: 50, width:
  view.frame.width - 32, height: 50)
  view.addSubview(loginButton)
```

Now, if you build and launch your application you will see **Continue with Facebook** button as in the following screenshot:

Figure 19: iOS application after adding the Facebook authentication button

Things start to look much better now; if you click on the button you will be redirected using Safari to the authorization page as in the following screenshot:

Figure 20: Facebook account, Facebook application authorization

Please note that there are two scenarios when you click the login button: the first one is when you have the actual Facebook application installed on your phone, the second is when you don't have it. When you don't, you will be redirected using Safari so you can complete this task.

Now, let's implement the connection delegates. Make sure you implement the `FBSDKLoginButtonDelegate` protocol by implementing `didCompleteWithResult:error` and `loginButtonDidLogOut` accordingly, as the following code represents:

```
func loginButton(_ loginButton: FBSDKLoginButton!,
didCompleteWith result:
 FBSDKLoginManagerLoginResult!, error: Error!) {
    if let error = error {
      print(error.localizedDescription)
```

```
        return
    }
    print("logging in ..")
}
 func loginButtonDidLogOut(_ loginButton:
 FBSDKLoginButton!) {
   print("logging out ..")
 }
```

Now simply build and run your project; you will notice something different with your connection button. The result will be the presence of the **Log out** button (Figure 21).

Figure 21: Facebook button after executing the authentication delegate

That's cool for now, it's mainly the normal behavior when you want to add Facebook within any iOS application, but the Firebase side was not uploaded yet, so let's see how we can add it.

Inside `didCompleteWithResult:error,` just add the following code for error checking:

```
let credential =
FacebookAuthProvider.credential(withAccessToken:
 FBSDKAccessToken.current().tokenString)
   Auth.auth().signIn(with: credential) { (user,
error) in
      if let error = error {
      print(error.localizedDescription)
      return
   }
let alert = UIAlertController(title: "Logged in !",
message: user?.displayName as String?,
 preferredStyle: UIAlertControllerStyle.alert)
alert.addAction(UIAlertAction(title: "Click", style:
UIAlertActionStyle.default, handler: nil))
self.present(alert, animated: true, completion: nil)
   }
```

Now simply build and launch your application, click on the Facebook login button, and once the authentication operation is done, check your Firebase project console; you will see your new user present there.

 You might experience some problems with this process during development with your terminal, but the code and process are very operational during production when you test on a real device.

How it works...

The process behind the Firebase/Facebook connection is straightforward and it has two steps:

1. You will need to create the UI and the connection behavior of your application in the exact same way for a Firebase free application. This means that you need to download the SDKs, create the connection button, and wire up the behavior underneath it, and also implement the `FBSDKLoginButtonDelegate` with its two functions.

2. Then once those delegate functions are implemented, the Firebase behavior will kick in, exploiting the behavior that was just created and connecting to Facebook, giving us some profile metadata to exploit.

Generating a crash report using Firebase Crash Report

Knowing when your application crashes and having a log of when that happens can save your application from having all sort of crashing/bad app availability comments over the Play/App Stores. Firebase, with the awesome Crash Report functionality, allows us to do just that, so let's explore how we can make that happen in Android/iOS.

How to do it...

Let us first look at how this recipe is implemented in Android:

1. In order to use this awesome feature, you will need to install some dependencies first, so head directly to your `build.gradle` file and add the following line to the dependencies:

    ```
    compile 'com.google.firebase:firebase-crash:11.0.4'
    ```

2. Now, simply save and hit that **sync** button; it will download the library and configure your Android project accordingly.

3. Please note that in Android, the crash reports are codeless out of the box, but we can make such a flow more human friendly by adding the following line:

```
FirebaseCrash.log("[*] I've got something wrong !");
// Or
FirebaseCrash.report("<Exception/Crash>");
```

We can use the log to log the event or the report in order to report crashes that we might not know the source of, and all those reports will take less than a second to reach out to Firebase!

Using Firebase Crash Reports can save you tons of frustration and pointless working hours, and can you help fix those nasty bugs in no time.

Now we will go through the implementation of this recipe in iOS:

1. As in any new feature we introduce in Firebase, installing the right library is a must, and that's why we need to install the iOS Crash Library using the usual flow with our `Podfile` file. Simply copy/paste this line and add it underneath your Pods:

```
pod 'Firebase/Crash'
```

2. After that, in your terminal, type the following command:

```
~> pod install
```

3. This will simply install all the needed dependencies and configure your project with the new library. Now let's do some quick configuration in order to make sure that everything is okay to host the crash reports functionality, simply because we want a human-readable crash report instead of the one generated by Xcode.

Please go over to your Firebase console and follow these steps:

1. Go to **Overview** | **SERVICE ACCOUNTS** | **Crash Reporting** as shown in the following figure:

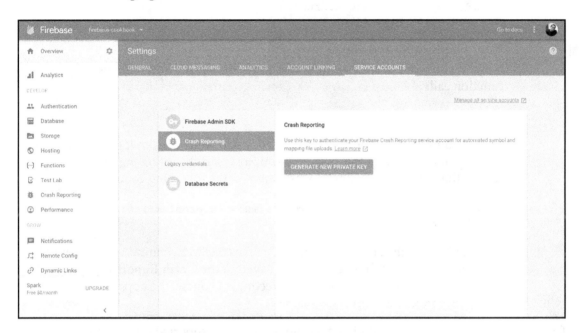

Figure 22: Firebase project service account section

2. Click on the **GENERATE NEW PRIVATE KEY** button so you can download the private JSON file and include it somewhere in your application; make sure that you won't commit it to Github or any git-based system for the public.

3. Create a new **Build Phase** and select the **Run Script** option. In it, add the following content:

```
GOOGLE_APP_ID=1:<Google App ID>
"${PODS_ROOT}"/FirebaseCrash/upload-sym
<Configuration File Path>
```

4. Now simply build and you're set to go!

5. Now, if you want to start sending crash reports, simply add the following function call:

```
fatalError()
```

6. Now, you might wonder how we can set or add some custom logs or text while sending our logs. Well, the answer is simple; insert the following line before calling the `fatalError` function, as shown in the following code:

```
FirebaseCrashMessage("[*] Huston ! we've a problem")
fatalError()
```

Now, notice that the crash report usually takes one to two minutes in order to be sent, and all those crash reports will be saved in the **Crash Reporting** section inside your Firebase project console, selecting, of course, the app you're developing from the drop-down above.

Congratulations! You've successfully added Firebase Crash Report abilities within your application. All you need now is to simply add this whenever it's needed and you will save yourself tons of pointless working hours.

Adding dynamic behavior using Firebase Remote Config in Android

Sometimes, it would be nice to change your application in a magical way; when I say magical I mean in a configuration-based way. That will help significantly customize the look and feel of our application without changing the code/user interface behind the app and push back to the app store, waiting for the store approval and then make it public to users.

Firebase Remote Config offers an optimal way to make UI changes on the fly, based on some pre-saved and fetched configuration objects. It's the best, easiest, and fastest way to make changes on the fly without re-uploading your application to the store and having to wait all that time to make a tiny change to your UI or your UX.

The use cases can differ from one application to another. Let's suppose you're building an e-commerce application. Such an application will definitely be shipped with special pages for the holidays or the Black Friday event. You just don't want to change your application during the holidays or simply ship a new update for each and every holiday. Firebase Remote Config offers us the best and right solution, so let's see how we can integrate and use this in our application.

In this recipe, we're going to see how we can implement the Firebase Remote Config functionality over Android, but before that, let's see what need to do first before we dig inside the code.

Getting ready

Everything starts with the setup process, so let's install the Firebase Remote Config Library in our Android project. Simply open up your application with Android Studio and simply copy/paste this line in your `build.gradle` files within the dependencies section, underneath your already-installed libraries:

```
compile 'com.google.firebase:firebase-config:11.4.2'
```

Now, simply save and sync your Android project and the gradle build system will install the library and configure your project accordingly.

How to do it...

Let's see how we can use Firebase Remote Config within the scope of our application. What I will do is to test if the Facebook login will affect my user base in any way, and if such functionality will help me get more users for my application. Doing something like this in the past would require me to create a complete build, and test and finally upload my application to the App Store—a tedious and painful process just to remove a single line of code.

Besides, we won't have the option of changing our options on the fly, so let's see the steps needed to do so.

First, here's a glimpse of my Android application—it supports two authentication methods, email, and Facebook:

Figure 23: Android application before adding Firebase Remote Config

Now, head over to your `Login Activity` class, and add the following declaration:

```
Boolean doISupportFacebookAuth;
private FirebaseRemoteConfig rConfig =
FirebaseRemoteConfig.getInstance();
```

Next, within the `onCreate` method, introduce the following:

```
rConfig.setConfigSettings(new
FirebaseRemoteConfigSettings.Builder()
  .setDeveloperModeEnabled(true)
  .build());
```

This simply kicks in Remote Config within the application, and since we're still in development, let's enable the Developer Mode so we can work freely. Then we simply call the build method to finalize everything.

Next, let's transform the Firebase UI logic we're using to create the lovely, easy login interface:

```
if(doISupportFacebookAuth) {
      startActivityForResult(
         AuthUI.getInstance()
            .createSignInIntentBuilder()
            .setAvailableProviders(
            Arrays.asList(new
 AuthUI.IdpConfig.Builder(AuthUI.EMAIL_PROVIDER)
.build(),
 new AuthUI.IdpConfig.Builder(
 AuthUI.FACEBOOK_PROVIDER).build())).build(),
     RC_SIGN_IN);
   } else {
    startActivityForResult(
    AuthUI.getInstance()
            .createSignInIntentBuilder()
            .setAvailableProviders(
             Arrays.asList(new
  AuthUI.IdpConfig.Builder(AuthUI.EMAIL_PROVIDER)
  .build())).build(),
    RC_SIGN_IN);
  }
```

What I'm doing here is simple. I'm testing if the `doISupportFacebookAuth` value is `true` or `false`; if it's `true` I will simply add Facebook authentication, or else I will simply strip it out. Nothing fancy here.

Now, let's see how we can add the default for `doISupportFacebookAuth`. Before our Firebase UI code, add the following:

```
HashMap<String, Object> defaultValues = new
HashMap();
defaultValues.put("doISupportFacebookAuth", true);
rConfig.setDefaults(defaultValues);
```

In the preceding code, we're simply passing a `HashMap` that will hold our values, and simply passing that `HashMap` to our config using the `setDefaults()` method.

Next, to retrieve that value, simply add the following above your authentication if statement:

```
doISupportFacebookAuth =
rConfig.getBoolean("doISupportFacebookAuth");
```

So now our application will launch in its default state, and the Facebook button will show because we didn't add yet the field value to our Firebase project console.

 Any remote value needs to have mainly two values, one locally within the default state and the other inside your **Firebase Remote Config** section.

Let's see how we can add that value to our console. Head to Project **Console** | **Remote Config** and click on the **ADD YOUR FIRST PARAMETER** button. You will be greeted with the following model:

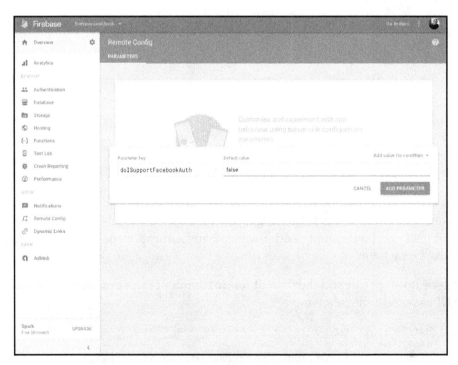

Figure 24: Facebook Remote Config parameter adding section

Your field name should be exactly the same as the previous code. Insert the field name and value, then click **ADD PARAMETER**.

Now let's see how we can fetch those values. In your code, add the following:

```
final Task<Void> fetch = rConfig.fetch(0); //Cache
experation time, 0 value = Keep on fetching.
fetch.addOnSuccessListener(this, new
 OnSuccessListener<Void>() {
   @Override
   public void onSuccess(Void aVoid) {
   rConfig.activateFetched();
   }
});
```

You *must* call the `activateFetched()` method, as without it the local values won't get updated.

What this will do is simply make a request to your Firebase project remote configuration and return back those values you've added.

Next, click on the **PUBLISH CHANGES** button so you can deploy your changes:

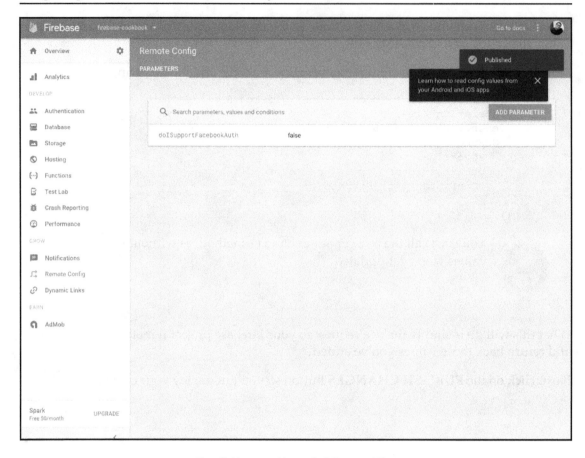

Figure 25: After a successful remote Config Parameter addition

Now, simply exit the application and enter it again; what you will notice is that your application will head directly to email authentication with no Facebook login button available. If you want that to come back, simply change the value in your Firebase project console to `true`, and you're set to go back to your normal state.

How it works...

Let's explain what just happened:

1. First, we started by adding our dependencies to our application to our `build.gradle` file. This is important, as, without it, the functionality won't work.

2. We defined/initialized our remote config object and turned the developer mode on. This changes during production, but since we're still in development we need to keep it on.
3. We set a HashMap with our default values and passed it to our Remote Config default values.
4. Since our value was a Boolean we used the `getBoolean()` function with the field name we wanted to retrieve.
5. We set that field name and put its value in our Firebase project Console Remote config section.
6. After that, we fetched that value and used the `activateFetched()` method; without this, our local Remote Config wouldn't be updated.
7. Then after that, we published the values from our console. With that, we were finished with the requirement to integrate Remote Config within our Android application.

We've successfully added the Remote Config to our Android application.

Adding dynamic behavior using Firebase Remote Config in iOS

In this recipe, we're going to implement the Firebase Remote Config in an iOS context, and as an example, we're going to cover how we effectively use the Firebase Remote Config API's to create somehow an A/B testing for our Google OAuth button. This will allow us to activate it or disable it right from the Firebase Remote Config section within your Firebase project console.

Getting ready

Since Firebase is highly modular, the Remote Config has its very own library, so let's install it. In your `Podfile`, add the following line underneath your dependencies:

```
pod 'Firebase/RemoteConfig'
```

Now, in your terminal, simply type the following command:

```
~> pod install
```

This command will go and install the Firebase Remote Config library and download all its dependencies and configure your iOS application accordingly.

How to do it...

After installing the needed dependencies, let's start adding our logic to support the needed behavior. Within our application, I would like to test if adding Google Sign-in will affect my user base or not, so what I'm doing is integrating Firebase Remote Config within my application so I simply have a dynamic render for my testing purposes:

Figure 26: iOS application before adding the Firebase Remote Config

Head directly to your `LoginViewController` and import Firebase, if you haven't done that already:

```
import Firebase
```

Now, within the `viewDidLoaded()` function, we will need to implement the Firebase Remote Config in order to initialize a default set of values. These values will control mainly our user interface in this context, and the information can be passed either through a dictionary of [`String: NSObject`] or via a `plist` file.

For our current usage, we will use the dictionary approach for easy implementation:

```
//Default values Dict
let defaultConfigs = ["supportGoogleLogin" : true ]
```

Now, pass this dict to the Firebase Remote Config, as follows:

```
RemoteConfig.remoteConfig().setDefaults(defaultConfigs
as [String : NSObject])
```

Now, let's see how we can fetch the remote values that we will add shortly, use the following function call, it will have a cache expiration time and a simple `completeHandler`:

```
RemoteConfig.remoteConfig().fetch(\
withExpirationDuration: 0, completionHandler:
 {[unowned self] (status, error) in
    if let error = error {
     print("Huston we've a problem : \(error)")
     return
  }

 print("Huston , al Goodt    ")
 RemoteConfig.remoteConfig().activateFetched()
 self.checkLoginButtonPresence() //to update our UI.
})
```

Now, in the code, I've called the Remote config `fetch:withExpiration`, giving it a value of zero, which translates to an instant check.

Now, this approach will throttle our device heavily. Why? Because we're constantly checking for the new values. This is not recommended for production, so in order to add more to that throttling, let's activate the developer mode by adding the following lines of code above the fetch request:

```
let developerSettings =
RemoteConfigSettings(developerModeEnabled: true) //
This should be remove while going to prod.
RemoteConfig.remoteConfig().configSettings =
developerSettings!
```

With that, we're safe enough to test it, but remember to remove it once you're in production.

Now, let's talk about the content of `checkLoginButtonPresence()` which will simply update our UI:

```
func checkLoginButtonPresence() {
  let supportGoogleLogin =
RemoteConfig.remoteConfig().configValue(forKey:
"supportGoogleLogin").boolValue
  if(supportGoogleLogin) {
      //Facebook Login
      let loginButton = FBSDKLoginButton()
      loginButton.frame = CGRect(x: 16, y: 50, width
      view.frame.width - 32, height: 50)
      view.addSubview(loginButton)
      loginButton.delegate = self
      //Google sign in
      let googleBtn = GIDSignInButton()
      googleBtn.frame =  CGRect(x: 16, y: 111, width:
      view.frame.width - 32, height: 50)
      view.addSubview(googleBtn)
      GIDSignIn.sharedInstance().uiDelegate = self
      } else {
      //Facebook Login
      let loginButton = FBSDKLoginButton()
      loginButton.frame = CGRect(x: 16, y: 50, width:
      view.frame.width - 32, height: 50)
      view.addSubview(loginButton)
      loginButton.delegate = self
  }
}
```

In the preceding code, we're doing two things:

1. Retrieving the value from Firebase Remote Config using the `RemoteConfig.remoteConfig().configValue()` function and giving it the name of our property. We're also using `boolValue` to simply return our value as a Boolean.

2. We're checking based on the value of the properties and handling our UI accordingly.

Now, let's add our value to our Firebase Project console, in the **Remote Config** section:

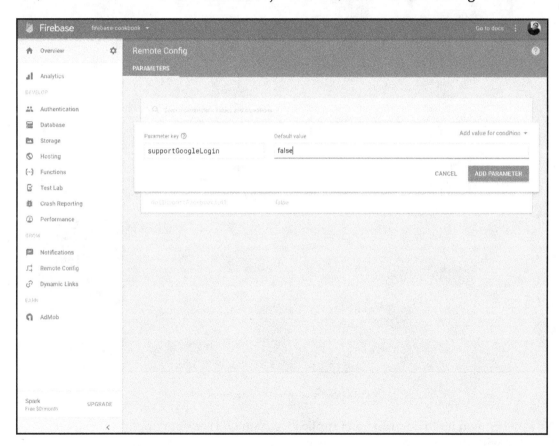

Figure 27: Adding the Firebase Remote Config parameter to our application

You must supply the exact same property name that you used in your code, or else it won't work.

After adding and saving it, click on the **PUBLISH CHANGES** button:

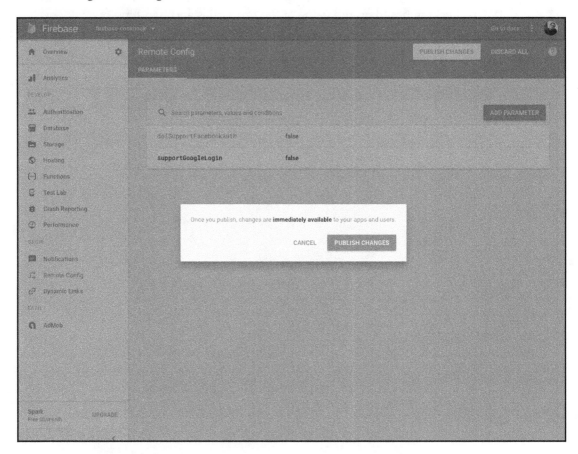

Figure 28: Publishing our newly added configuration parameter

Now, when you build and run your application, you will see your application already bundled with the new changes. If you want to test it, simply change the value in your console, publish it again, exit the application, and log it once again. Your modification will be applied.

How it works...

Let's explain what just happened:

1. First, we defined the default value that our application will use locally and simply passed that to our Firebase Remote Config object.
2. Then, we called the `fetch` method so we could retrieve all those values from our console project. and called the `activateFetched()` function so we could wire up everything together.
3. Because we're still in development and because we were afraid of our throttle modal, we added the developer settings so we could bypass that.
4. We retrieved the value we got and tested the potential of using the Google Sign-in button.
5. Finally, we set that property name over our Firebase project console and published it.

With that, we've successfully added a Remote Config to our iOS application.

12
Hack Application's Growth

In this chapter, we'll cover the following recipes:

- Implementing sending/receiving app invite on Android/iOS
- Implementing topic subscription on Android/iOS

Introduction

Growth is the topic of the age. It is the result of accumulated effects, techniques, and many hours of improvement that shall make your application indispensable. In this chapter, we'll see and implement some Firebase magic in order to make our application features as proved to be awesome. We'll cover topics beyond sending a simple notification, basically speaking about topic subscription over both iOS and Android. As users love to share, we'll see how we can get used to the Firebase app invite functionalities and make our application's user base go beyond expectations. It'll be exciting, so let's start hacking.

Implementing sending/receiving app invite in Android/iOS

Generally, people tend to share the things that they find interesting, from a cool cats video to an article about Firebase--maybe this is just me. Furthermore, since sharing is widespread, people nowadays tend to expect to find App invite functionality within apps. It'll be a win-win relationship because if users have the application within their ecosystem, that would be great as they navigate directly using deep linking; otherwise, they'll install it, so we're winning new leads with each message.

The message format can be diverse. We've two options email and SMS. With SMS, the message will contain a link by the Firebase dynamic links; this link generated will be preserved and saved over installation time in the memory. This means that even if the users don't use the application installed on their phones, once the setup process is done, the app will redirect using deep links and navigate directly to the screen with the desired content.

Since we'll implement the functionality on both iOS and Android systems, let's see how we can configure our development project to host the app invite functionality.

Getting ready

The requirements for implementing app invites in Android will be discussed first. Then, we will move to the requirements in iOS:

1. Fire up your Android Studio and go directly to your `build.gradle` file and add the following line in the dependencies section:

   ```
   compile 'com.google.firebase:firebase-
   invites:11.0.4'
   ```

2. Now simply save and sync your build. After that, Android Studio will download and configure your build accordingly and technically, we're done.

 For in-depth information about how to configure/integrate Firebase within your Android project, check `Chapter 1`, *Firebase - Getting Started*.

Now that we are done with Android preparation, let's now move to checking the requirements for app invite implementation in iOS:

1. In your iOS application project, edit your Podfile and add the following line underneath your Pods:

   ```
   pod 'Firebase/Invites'
   ```

2. Now, save the file and type the following command in your Terminal:

   ```
   ~> pod install
   ```

This command will go and download the library and the other dependencies that app invites rely on and configure your project build with it. You've successfully configured your iOS project with this.

For in-depth reading on how to configure/integrate Firebase within your iOS project, check Chapter 1, *Firebase - Getting Started*.

How to do it...

Following the method we used in the previous section, here we will deal with the implementation of the recipe in Android first:

1. In order to make this happen, the Android ecosystem has a user experience flow. Whenever we want to share something, we launch a dialog or Intent. This intent will allow us to choose how to send our app invite.

Intents over Android are a way to interact with other applications via message sending in order to request functionalities; for example, we launch an intent for sending an SMS. This will simply launch the default messaging app and take whatever parameter we want, such as the content of the text itself.

2. Now, let's see how we can make the functionality happen. Let's suppose that we have a news app with a material card; this card will have a menu button to share content. The following code represents the functionality behind the workflow:

```
private void shareContent() {
    Intent intent = new
    AppInviteInvitation.IntentBuilder(getString(
    /*Intent Name*/))
        .setMessage(/*Message Content*/)
        .setDeepLink(Uri.parse(/*Deep Link*/))
        .build();
    startActivityForResult(intent, REQUEST_INVITE);
}
```

Now that we've finished the code behind the sending process, what we will need next is to simply execute everything, choose the sending manner, and simply see the Firebase magic.

1. The perfect plan is not finished yet; our application won't recognize any of the work we did, and the message won't have any meaning. Let's add the following code to the application's onCreate method:

```
FirebaseDynamicLinks.getInstance().getDynamicLink(
    getIntent())
```

```
                .addOnSuccessListener(this, new
        OnSuccessListener<PendingDynamicLinkData>() {
        @Override
        public void onSuccess(PendingDynamicLinkData data) {
            if (data == null) {
                //No Data, do nothing !
                 return;
                }
                Uri deepLink = data.getLink();
                // Extract invite
                FirebaseAppInvite invite =
              FirebaseAppInvite.getInvitation(data);
                    if (invite != null) {
                     String invitationId =
                     invite.getInvitationId();
                     }
          // TODO: perform Deep linking
              }
          })
          .addOnFailureListener(this, new
           OnFailureListener() {
            @Override
            public void onFailure(@NonNull Exception e)
        {
            //TODO: Handle exception.
              }
        });
```

With that, we're done!

Now for those working with iOS, let's look at the implementation of this recipe, which will teach you the execution of sending and receiving app invites.

The process of the invitation sending can differ from one application to another, but everything starts with a tap of a button. So, let's configure our IBAction and start the process of sending the app invite:

```
@IBAction func sendInvite(_ sender: AnyObject) {
  if let invite = <strong>Invites.inviteDialog() {
    invite.setInviteDelegate(self)
    invite.setMessage("/*Message Content*/")
    invite.setTitle("/*Invite Title*/")
    invite.setDeepLink("/*Deep Link*/")
    invite.open()
  }
}
```

Before this, your class needs to be signed using the `FIRInviteDelegate` protocol, as follows:

```
class NewViewController : ViewController,
    InviteDelegate {
}
```

Now, if we want things to be more user-friendly, we can add a simple alert to show that an invite has been sent using the `inviteFinished()` function, as the following code shows:

```
func inviteFinished(withInvitations invitationIds:
  [Any], error: Error?) {
  if let error = error {
    let alert = UIAlertController(title: "Error",
    message: "a problem has occured while sending
    your invitation",
  preferredStyle: UIAlertControllerStyle.alert)
  alert.addAction(UIAlertAction(title: "OK",
  style: UIAlertActionStyle.default, handler: nil))
  self.present(alert, animated: true, completion:nil)
  } else {
  let alert = UIAlertController(title: "Success",
  message: "Your invitation has been successfully
      sent", preferredStyle:
        UIAlertControllerStyle.alert)
  alert.addAction(UIAlertAction(title: "OK", style:
    UIAlertActionStyle.default, handler: nil))
  self.present(alert, animated: true, completion:
    nil)
  }
}
```

This will make your app invite ready. Now, start setting your invite content and deep links and start sending those engaging invites; your growth will never be the same.

Since we've successfully sent the invitation, now we need to add some custom invite reception management to our application. So, let's see how we can make that possible:

```
func application(_ application: UIApplication, open
url: URL, options: [UIApplicationOpenURLOptionsKey :
  Any])-> Bool {
    return self.application(application, open: url,
    sourceApplication:
    options[UIApplicationOpenURLOptionsKey
    .sourceApplication] as? String, annotation: "")
  }

  func application(_ application: UIApplication,
```

```
     open url: URL, sourceApplication: String?,
       annotation: Any) -> Bool {
     if let invite = Invites.handle(url,
       sourceApplication:sourceApplication,
       annotation:annotation) as? ReceivedInvite {
       //TODO: Handle invite reception.
       return true
     }

     return GIDSignIn.sharedInstance().handle(url,
       sourceApplication: sourceApplication,
       annotation: annotation)
   }
```

You won't be able to send an invite unless your users are connected to their Google account. To learn how you can support such functionality, refer to `Chapter 13`, *Adding Analytics and Maximizing Earnings*.

How it works...

Now, let's explain the preceding code:

1. We're building a new Intent using the `AppInviteInvitation` Firebase app intent library.
2. We're setting a couple of options:
    1. The `setMessage()` method: This method will add the app invite message's content. This content will work on both SMS and email. We do have another option for email sending--using the `setEmailHtmlContent` method; this one will let us provide custom HTML content for our email; this can be really customizable.
    2. The `setDeepLink()` method: This method will let us add the deep link. When provided, this will make a custom and add it to your app invite SMS/email.
    3. Finally, we're starting the activity with the intent we built.
3. In the `onCreate` method, we're simply listening to that call. Once we successfully receive an invite, we'll just perform the required behavior from deep linking and invite extraction.

We will now switch to how the recipe works for iOS.

Let's explain what just happened:

1. We started by setting our user interface, moving on to simply wiring the sending process.
2. Within the delegate invocation, we set the message, title, and the deep link, and then simply opened the invite so that we can select the person we want to send an invite to.
3. In the `inviteFinished()` function, we set what will happen after we successfully sent the invite. In our case, it will be a simple alert; it's up to you to set the right behavior.
4. We wired the normal behavior once we receive an invite. This behavior needs to be in place and will launch automatically once your application receives an invite; if the application exists, you will simply follow that deep link. Otherwise, you will be guided to the app store so that you can download the application. However, once you do so, and the application starts on your iOS device, you will be navigated directly; this is important so that you can preserve your application's UX.

Implementing topic subscription in Android/ iOS

Topic subscription is self-explanatory. Sometimes within a news app, you won't want to have a notification for all the news. Maybe you want to get the latest and most important news, maybe you want to know today's top games, or you might just want to know your favorite team major news on a daily basis; such an experience is present, available, and doable using the Firebase topic subscription API.

Now, let's see how we can provide such an experience to our users, knowing that the UI can differ from one application to another. Maybe you've got a dashboard for an important news, or sports, or weather, but you might go deeper, providing custom titles or topics.

 Firebase topic subscription is smart enough to create a new topic if the topic you want to subscribe to is not registered to a custom topic that Firebase or your application handles.

How to do it...

We will now take a look at applying topic subscription using this recipe for those working with Android:

1. The new Firebase API makes the process really easy; in order to subscribe to any topic, we just execute the following line of code, which simply translates to a button click or a switch on your settings pages:

```
FirebaseMessaging.getInstance().subscribeToTopic(
"top-news");
```

2. Now, if you want to unsubscribe from a given topic, you can just execute the following line of code:

```
FirebaseMessaging.getInstance().unsubscribeFromTopic("top-news");
```

Congratulations! You've successfully subscribed to the `top-news` topic on your application. What's left is to simply manage the sending process from your backend, and you will receive all the push notification messages once they've been sent from your backend.

As always, the next part of the recipe will be about working on the implementation of topic subscription on iOS:

1. The process of iOS is also straightforward. Simply imagine having a dashboard for all the major topics that we might have on our Firebase application. However, keep in mind that the creation and subscription to the topics are dynamically created; if the topic isn't found, Firebase simply creates it.

2. Let's see how we can subscribe/unsubscribe to topics:

```
FIRMessaging.messaging().subscribeToTopic("top-news");
```

3. Now, if we want to unsubscribe, we just need to execute the following line:

```
FIRMessaging.messaging().unsubscribeFromTopic("top-news")
```

Now it's up to your backend to send that topic-based notification, and your application will be notified based on the topic itself.

How it works...

The concept behind this feature is quite neat; what we want to do is to simply to send a theme-based notification to stop the notification spamming. While doing that, we have two functionalities that we need to keep in mind:

- Subscribing to a specific topic: This functionality will save the required information of a given device, speaking mainly about the registration ID or the unique token that identifies your device and grouping it with other tokens that requested the same topic. From now on, when the application server sends, whether it's a time-based notification or an instant one, it will mainly be for the user who just asked for the theme or topic itself, not for the overall users.
- The second part is users unsubscribing, which simply means that a given user will delete their unique id from the set or group of tokens that will get the theme/topic-based notification. So, if we unsubscribe from the "top-news" topic, we won't get any notifications that are related to that topic.

The most suitable place for such functionalities is on a specific dashboard where you hold all your topics for easy and fast access for both subscribing and unsubscribing.

13
Adding Analytics and Maximizing Earnings

In this chapter, we'll cover the following recipes:

- Integrating Firebase analytics into Android/iOS applications
- Implementing event logging on Android/iOS
- Implementing user properties for data and audience filtering
- Integrating Firebase AdMob with Android/iOS application
- Implementing Firebase AdMob banner ads on Android/iOS
- Implementing Firebase AdMob native ads express on Android/iOS
- Implementing AdMob ads targeting

Introduction

Congrats! You have finished working on that new shiny application of yours. You are probably now seeking to get more information, know your user's preferences, and why not generate some money from the app as a treat for your hard work.

Firebase offers that and more. With an end-to-end analytics system, AdMob integration, and more, it is what I love to call the next pre-finished working app integration you need to manage, so you can ensure you're hearing feedback and listening to your users at least in an indirect way.

In this chapter, we're going to see how we can manage and implement analytic and AdMob campaigns within your Firebase mobile application.

Integrating Firebase analytics into Android/iOS applications

You've probably heard about Google analytics before. It's the best friend of developers and marketers when it comes to getting metrics and gathering non-intrusive data about their application's users. For a long time, having such a powerful mobile platform was a dream, but now Firebase is offering that by providing you with both a very beautiful yet very informative dashboard that you can find over at your Firebase project console. Here's how our current Android Firebase powered application will look over at **Analytics**:

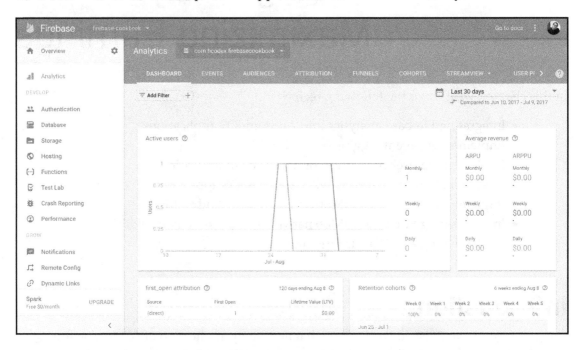

Figure 1: Firebase Analytics based on application section.

It will hold up everything from active users, to a total awesome map showing you where your users are coming from, to even the kind of mobile devices they are using, as well as the OS version. Also, with such integration, we can do more, such as logging events, errors, or getting the predefined user properties.

How to do it...

Let us first see how to configure Android applications:

1. Fire up your Android Studio, and head directly to your `build.gradle` file.
2. Add the following line underneath your already present dependencies:

   ```
   compile 'com.google.firebase:firebase-core:11.0.4'
   ```

3. Now simply save and sync, and Android Studio will simply download and configure your project accordingly!

Congrats! You've successfully configured your Android application to host Firebase analytics!

Now let us check how this is done for iOS:

We're using CocoaPods in order to download and build dependency trees within our iOS application:

1. Open up your Podfile and add the following line underneath your already present dependencies:

   ```
   pod 'Firebase/Core'
   ```

2. Now, in your terminal please type the following command:

   ```
   ~> pod install
   ```

This will go and download and configure our iOS application accordingly!

> Please check `Chapter 1`, *Firebase - Getting Started*, where we introduce configuring of an iOS application using CocoaPods and Firebase.

Congrats! You've successfully configured your IOS application to host Firebase analytics!

Implementing event logging on Android/iOS

Knowing that analytics start when your application starts sending basic information that you normally see on the dashboard, we can simply create another event. This would be an event that would suit our application's needs. Those analytics logs are free forever, so get creative with your logs or simply play it safe and use the Firebase default events and report them back.

Let's see how we can integrate those lovely, full of data events into our applications for both Android and iOS.

How to do it...

Let us first see how event logging is done on Android:

1. After you've successfully installed the library in your application and selected the required activity of class where you want to host your analytics within, start with a reference, just like everything in Firebase:

    ```
    private FirebaseAnalytics fireAnalytics;
    ```

2. Then in your onCreate method, grab the analytics instance via the following line:

    ```
    fireAnalytics = FirebaseAnalytics.getInstance(this);
    ```

3. Now after grabbing our working reference, let's send some logs.
4. After choosing the place where you want to send the valuable analytics info, simply add the following line via calling the logEvent() method:

    ```
    fireAnalytics.logEvent("cookbook_request", null);
    ```

5. This tracks the event without sending any further parameters of metadata. Now in order to do so, we simply bundle everything inside--well you guessed it--a bundle instance, where we can inject whatever we want. So let's see how we can make it happen using the following code snippet:

    ```
    Bundle bundle = new Bundle();
    bundle.putString("book_name", "Firebase Cookbook");
    bundle.putInt("book_quantity", 1);
      fireAnalytics.logEvent("cookbook_request", bundle);
    ```

Congrats! We're done! This information will be streamed live on our dashboard.

Next, we will see how event logging is done on iOS.

Suppose that you've configured all needed dependencies within the iOS application and also configured your application to host Firebase features, let's see how we can add those amazing analytics logs and reports to our application:

1. Let's suppose we want to log the book request and the quantity, then it would probably look similar to this code block:

```
Analytics.logEvent("cookbook_request", parameters: [
   "book_name": name as NSObject,
   "book_quantity": quanity as NSObject
   ])
```

2. This method injection can happen anywhere within your application as you wish. So pick the place you seek to include the data most and inject the data you want. They will all be present in the Project **Console** | **Analytics** section.

In these preceding recipes, we've shown how you can interact and integrate the Firebase analytics within our Android and iOS applications. Do not forget that the Firebase analytics is a 100% free and unlimited feature for logging and reporting with your application. So, go ahead and enjoy!

Implementing user properties for data and audience filtering

Suppose you want to find out people who like the new movies of Marvel or DC, or you want to discover the people who just like to eat pizza. The user properties section in your Firebase analytics section can give you up to 25 custom defined user properties.

Firebase already has some pre-predefined user properties, such as user gender, user country, and so on. You can get the list of all the predefined user properties from here: https://support.google.com/firebase/answer/6317486?hl=enref_topic=6317484.

Now let's define some user properties. It starts with selecting the wanted application--in my case, it's my Android application, but you can select any of the apps that use your Firebase project--and then adding the user property itself within the Firebase project console. To do so, simply head to your **Project Console** | **Analytics** | **USER PROPERTIES** tab and simply click on the **NEW USER PROPERTY** button. Then you can add both the **User property name** and property **Description** (*Figure 2*):

Figure 2: Adding a new Application based User property

Now simply hit the **CREATE** button and you're done!

The way shown in the preceding screenshot is the same for any application that uses your Firebase project, so if you have an Android application and an iOS one you will need to create a user property for both of them, which means you can have custom user properties in different ecosystems.

How to do it...

We will first learn about sending the metrics from Android:

1. Over at Android Studio, let's grab an instance from the Firebase analytics:

```
private FirebaseAnalytics myMoviesAnalytics;
myMoviesAnalytics = FirebaseAnalytics
.getInstance(this);
```

2. Now, let's suppose we have a Spinner dropdown where users can select their best movies of the year. Make sure your class implements the `OnItemSelectedListener` interface and then we need to override the `onItemSelected` method. This method will give us the index of the selected item from the list we provided to the `ArrayAdapter` when we created the Spinner list, it would look like this:

```
@Override
public void onItemSelected(
AdapterView<?> parent, View view, position, long id) {
  // [*] Getting the selected Item.
  String movie =
  parent.getItemAtPosition(position).toString();
  myMoviesAnalytics.setUserProperty(
  "favorite_movies", movie);
}
```

Once your users select their favorite movies, the Firebase instance will automatically push all the newly added values for all the users. By doing that we will have a base model to use in order to perform filtering requests from our **Analytics** dashboard.

3. To do that, simply click on the **Analytics** dashboard tab. Next move over to the **Add Filter** button, and after that select the **USER Property**, option. Now as you know it, you will find all your predefined and custom user properties. Once you picked the required choice, you will have a refreshed dashboard containing nothing but the user property value analytics that you collected early on.

Congrats! You've successfully configured your application to host custom user properties functionality.

Let us now move on to sending the metrics from iOS:

1. After configuring our wanted user property, let's add our movies list using nothing but a `TableController`. In order to get the selected movie now, let's implement the `didSelectRowAt` function within it so that we can get the selected movie name:

```
func tableView(_ tableView: UITableView,didSelectRowAt indexPath:
  IndexPath){
  let movie = self.moviesList(indexPath,row)
  Analytics.setUserProperty(movie, forName:
  "favorite_movies")
}
```

2. Now, we're halfway through. Once your users select the wanted movie from the list, the Firebase analytics method will directly add that value to our data model to filter through. In order to do that, go directly to your Firebase **Analytics** dashboard, click on the **Add filter**, and then select the **User Property** then select the wanted property and the wanted value. Then the dashboard will get automatically updated with the metrics you wanted for the given property value.

Congrats! You've successfully configured your iOS application to host custom user properties functionality.

Integrating Firebase AdMob with Android/iOS applications

AdMob makes your mobile application profitable using nothing but plain good old ads, the integration with Firebase that also provides other services like analytics and more advanced metrics makes Firebase and AdMob the perfect mix. So in the recipes, we're going to cover how we can integrate them into Android and iOS.

How to do it...

We will first discover how to integrate Firebase AdMob within our Android application:

1. Fire up Android Studio and open your `build.gradle` file. Add the following line underneath your already present dependencies:

```
compile 'com.google.firebase:firebase-ads:11.0.4'
```

2. Save and sync, and then, in Android Studio, go and download and install the needed dependencies and configure your project accordingly.
3. Now in your main activity Java class, initialize your AdMob integration with your AdMob app ID by adding the following line to your `onCreate` method:

```
MobileAds.initialize(this, "<Admob-App-Id>");
```

This line will allow your application to host the upcoming add that we're going to integrate shortly.

 In order to get the AdMob application ID, you will simply need to go to your Firebase Project **Console | AdMob** section clicking on the **SIGN UP FOR ADMOB** button and following the instructions from there.

Congrats! Your application is well configured to host the AdMob functionalities!

Let us now jump to integrating Firebase AdMob with iOS applications:

1. In order to integrate AdMob into your iOS application, edit your Podfile and add the following line underneath your dependencies:

```
pod 'Firebase/AdMob'
```

2. Now, simply go to your terminal and type the following line:

```
pod install
```

This command will download and configure your iOS project accordingly!

 Please check `Chapter 1`, *Firebase - Getting Started*, in case you're wondering how to configure your iOS project with CocoaPods.

3. Now we need to add one more line of code in order to fully configure our iOS application with AdMob. Go ahead to your `app delegate switch` class and add the following line of code within your `didFinishLaunchingWithOptions` function:

```
GADMobileAds.configure(withApplicationID: "<Admob-app-id>")
```

 In order to get the AdMob Application ID, you will need simply to go to your Firebase Project **Console** | **AdMob** section and click on the **SIGN UP FOR ADMOB** button and follow the instructions from there.

Congrats! Your application is well configured to host the AdMob functionalities.

Implementing Firebase AdMob banner ads on Android/iOS

They come in different sizes, can be put in different places, and they are really easy to be implemented. AdMob Banners offer that and more; let's see how we can add AdMob banner Ads to Android/iOS applications.

Getting ready

Please follow the instructions mentioned previously, on how you can download/configure your project with Firebase AdMob on your respective platform.

How to do it...

Let us first discover how Firebase AdMob banner ads are implemented in Android.

Over Android the process is divided into two parts:

- First part is where the ad will be located at
- Second is the banner configuration behind it with the respectable AdMob special ID

1. Let's start with the ad location in our UI by simply implementing the following code:

```
<com.google.android.gms.ads.AdView
  xmlns:ads="http://schemas.android.com/apk/res-auto"
    android:id="@+id/adView"
    android:layout_width="wrap_content"
    android:layout_height="wrap_content"
    android:layout_centerHorizontal="true"
    android:layout_alignParentBottom="true"
    ads:adSize="BANNER"
    ads:adUnitId="<Admob_Unit_Id>">
</com.google.android.gms.ads.AdView>
```

2. Now in our activity, let's add the following code:

```
protected void onCreate(Bundle savedInstanceState) {
    super.onCreate(savedInstanceState);
    setContentView(R.layout.activity_main);
    bannerRef = (AdView) findViewById(R.id.adView);
    AdRequest adRequest = new
    AdRequest.Builder().build();
    bannerRef.loadAd(adRequest);
}
```

With that, you're done!

The preceding code is for production-ready environments for real phone testing. In case you're using your Android Emulator, the ad won't show. To show it, simply add the `addTestDevice(AdRequest.DEVICE_ID_EMULATOR)` method call before your `AdRequest` build method one. Then you will able to showcase and test ads on your emulator.

We will now move ahead to the second part of the recipe which is implementing Firebase AdMob banner ads on iOS.

The process on iOS is straightforward, also divided into two parts:

1. The first part is the UI-based placement of the ad itself. Within your **Storyboard**, add a view and don't forget to set the wanted dimensions suitable for your needs. Also, you should not forget that you need to set the custom class of the view to `GADBannerView` as all the ads will be shown using this helper class.
2. Import `GoogleMobileAds`

3. The second part is showing your ads for real phone testing. Move over to your code and grab yourself an `IBOutlet` of that view. Next, in your `viewDidLoad()` function, add the following configurations:

```
@IBOutlet weak var bannerAddView: GADBannerView?
override func viewDidLoad() {
  super.viewDidLoad()
  bannerAdView.adUnitID = "<APP_UNIT_ID>"
  bannerAdView.rootViewController = self
  let request = GADRequest()
  bannerAdView.load(request)
}
```

With that, your application supports the AdMob banner ads. Congrats!

The preceding code is for production-ready environments for real phone testing, in case you're using your iOS emulator, the ad won't show. To show it simply add the following line:

```
request.testDevices = [kGADSimulatorID]
```

Adding the preceding line will make the testing available for all devices including the emulators.

How it works...

We will first see the implementation of this recipe in your Android applications.

As mentioned in the previous section of this recipe, the process is divided into two parts. Let's now see what we've just done.

Moving over to how the implementation was done in the UI section:

- We're calling for the Adview UI element related to the ad. In our case, we're using the banner one. This one will define the dimensions or the `adSize` of a given ad. Next, within the `adUnitID` property, we are adding the AdMob unit ID. You can get this ID from the Admob UI.

This ad unit ID is one per page or fragment. Just in case you want to showcase ads in every fragment of your application, simply create different ads and copy their respectable IDs accordingly.

It is time to see the part covered in the recipe which was concerned with the activity section of the application.

We're doing the following:

- Getting our UI reference.
- Creating and building our new Adrequest
- Simply loading the ad into the banner widget

With that, we're done with the Android portion!

Next in line is to see how the recipe worked for the implementation of Firebase AdMob banner ads in iOS.

In that section, we're doing the following:

1. Creating an AdMob with banner type and retrieving the ad unit ID related to the very same created ad.
2. Binding that to a view we created, and binding that view with the ad unit ID we created.
3. Finally, we loaded the Ad into our view. And as an extra step, we saw that we can add the `testDevices` array for all the supported devices we want our Ad to be tested at.

Implementing Firebase AdMob native ads express on Android/iOS

Whether there's a new application theme, new background, or a new event font that your shiny application both on Android or iOS can have, customizing ads to match your application is an available option. In this recipe, we're going to see how to make our application support the AdMob native ads express. So let's get to it!

Getting ready

Before we start, please follow the instructions mentioned previously on how to download/configure your project with Firebase AdMob on your respective platform.

Also before performing any coding on our application side, we will need to create the ad unit with the needed style. Remember, the native ads express lets you customize ads based on your applications look and like. All these styles can be applied by using nothing but pure CSS.

The following steps are applicable to every application you have. No matter if it's an Android application or an iOS application, the process is similar and straightforward. So let's see how we can manage to create our very own ad express:

1. Navigate to your AdMob console, and choose the application you're working on.
2. Click on **ADD AD UNIT** (*Figure 3*):

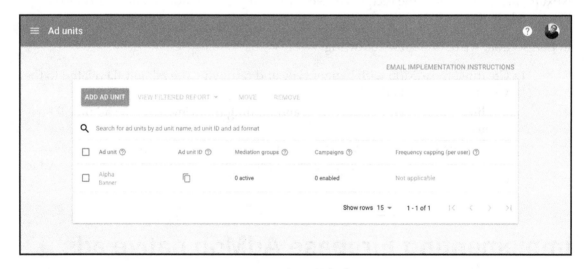

Figure 3: Adding new Ad Unit.

3. Once you're inside, click on **Native** and you will be introduced to the page shown in the following screenshot. Then click on the **GET STARTED** button (*Figure 4*):

Figure 4: Post AdMob native ads creation.

4. Next, you will need to select the size of your ad depending on your application needs (*Figure 5*):

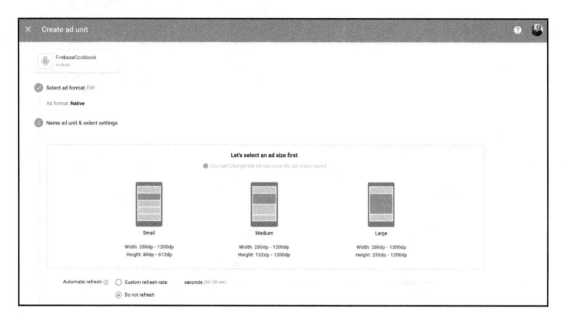

Figure 5: Native Ad size selection.

5. Afterwards, pick the design of your choice, and you can customize that as well (*Figure 6*):

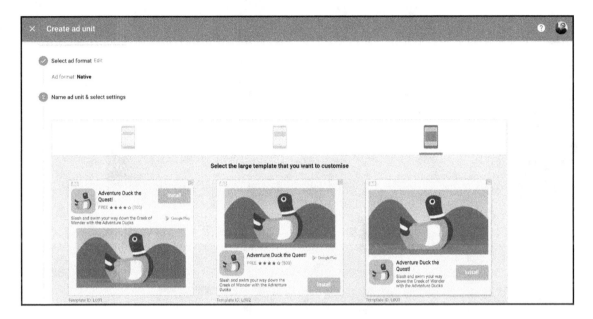

Figure 6: Native Ad template and Interface customization.

6. Finally, to start hacking with CSS, don't forget to add your ad unit name and hit the **Save** button to create your ad (*Figure 7*):

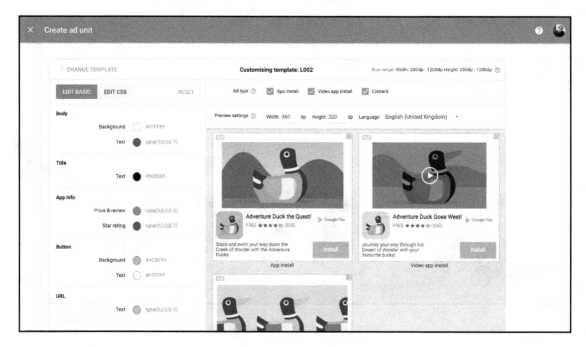

Figure 7: Changing the CSS based rules of our Native Ad template.

And hence, we're done with the configuration part of our ad.

 The preceding process needs to be done in case you have multiple apps. So in case you have an Android application and an iOS application, you will need to do a similar process to support both ecosystems.

How to do it...

We will first learn about implementing Firebase AdMob native ads express on Android and then we will move to iOS.

For Android:

1. There is only a minimal integration that we need to do with our code base to get started with native ads express on Android. Pretty much like the banner ad, we'll need to reserve a place for this ad on our UI!

2. Over the activity that you want, type the following code in your XML UI code:

```
<com.google.android.gms.ads.NativeExpressAdsView
   android:id="@+id/nativeExpressAd"
   android:layout_width="wrap_content"
   android:layout_height="wrap_content"
   ads:adSize="400x400"
   ads:adUnitId="<Admob_Unit_Id>">
</com.google.android.gms.ads.NativeExpressAdsView>
```

3. Now head to the Java code of your activity and type the following code lines for the next step:

```
protected void onCreate(Bundle savedInstanceState) {
super.onCreate(savedInstanceState);
setContentView(R.layout.activity_main);
NativeExpressAdView nativeExpress =
  (NativeExpressAdView) findViewById(
          R.id.nativeExpressAd);
  AdRequest adRequest = new
  AdRequest.Builder().build();
  nativeExpress.loadAd(adRequest);
}
```

With that, you're set to go. Just build your application, launch it, and enjoy your new native express ad!

The process of iOS is straightforward, and is also divided into two parts:

1. We start with the placement of the ad itself. Within your storyboard, add a view and give it the needed dimensions, and then finally set the custom class of the view to GADNativeExpressAdView. With this all your ads will be shown using this helper class.

2. Over your code, grab yourself an IBOutlet of that view. In your viewDidLoad() function, add the following configurations:

```
@IBOutlet weak var nativeAddView: GADNativeExpressAdView?
 override func viewDidLoad() {
 super.viewDidLoad()
  nativeAddView.adUnitID = "<APP_UNIT_ID>"
```

```
        nativeAddView.rootViewController = self
        nativeAddView.load(GADRequest())
    }
```

And believe it or not, that was it, you're set to go!

How it works...

It is time to discuss what just happened in the previous section:

1. We created our custom ad and customized it using nothing but simple CSS. After making sure that everything is great and suitable to our needs, we save it and take the AdUnitId that represents it.
2. We're creating the UI related to both ecosystems, which are Android and iOS, and we are placing it in the places we want to, within our application.
3. Depending on our supported ecosystem, we're showcasing the native express ad accidentally.

Congrats! Your application now supports the native express ad functionality.

Implementing AdMob ads targeting

An application can know diversity in a user's gender, age, locations, and more. Targeting your users based on many factors can significantly improve our user experience within our application. In this recipe, we're going to see how we can add just that to our Android and iOS applications.

Getting ready

Please follow the instructions mentioned previously on how to download/configure your project with Firebase AdMob on your respective platform.

How to do it...

Let us first see how ad targeting is implemented in Android:

1. The idea is to add the new filtering metadata to the `AdRequest` builder object and use methods such as `setGender()` for gender specification, `getLocation()` for specifying the location, and more.

2. Such configuration is applied in every case and scenario. Despite your Ad type, the idea is similar, so for simple implementation, the code will look like the following:

```
AdRequest request = new AdRequest.Builder()
    .setGender(AdRequest.GENDER_MALE)
    .build();
adView.loadAd(request);
```

`AdView` represents your ad reference on whether it's going to be a banner or mediation video or an event. Even for all other types of ads that we didn't cover within the scope of this book, the concept is the same.

We will now move on to how this is implemented in iOS:

- The concept of iOS is also fairly easy. All you have to do is add more metadata to the `GADRequest` and modify the enums present there, from gender to birthday. So let's see how we can implement it:

```
let request = GADRequest()
request.gender = .male
adView.loadRequest(request)
```

`adView` here is the view component that you've already created and grabbed an IBOutlet of. It can be a banner or any other type of ads that `Admob` support.

How it works...

Let's discuss what happened in the preceding code block:

1. We've created an ad and passed more metadata using the supported enums.
2. We then loaded the AdMob request into our ad view.
3. Now, based on your application account configuration, the ad will be shown to only the male users of our applications only. The same thing can happen if you change it to female as well.

 You can check the supported gender within the enum from here for iOS: `https://developers.google.com/admob/ios/api/reference/Enums/GADGender`, and `;https://developers.google.com/android/reference/com/google/android/gms/ads/AdRequest.Builder` for Android.

Congrats! Your application now supports the ad targeting functionality.

Firebase Cloud FireStore

Over the past 6 years, Firebase's products evolved and with Google integration, Firebase powered by Google simply became more powerful than it had been before. Such power meant some limitations on current products, for instance, the beloved Realtime Database that hypothetically knew some scalability. Developers, a lot of times, found it confusing as to how they should use it to simply store data.

Firebase Cloud FireStore, powered by Google's powerful database infrastructure, provided a solution by providing scalability, flexibility, and data management. Here are its main power points and, its differences from the earlier model:

1. Compared to the old Realtime Database, when it comes to the look and feel of data schemas, Cloud FireStore is more organized and structured than the old model. This difference facilitates the way developers think and feel about how they store and use the data. That, on its own, it's a very remarkable change.
2. Within the scope of Database, Cloud FireStore is more robust and scalable than to the Realtime Database.
3. It has a powerful query system that was built for performance, which means you only get what you're looking for. It has a chainable robust query system that helps you get the data you want using just straightforward queries.

4. It provides total support in real time, which means everything that was presented at the Firebase summit will be real time.
    1. Pretty much like the Firebase Realtime Database, Cloud FireStore supports offline functionalities using service workers over the web app and other techniques to keep your data synced while working. This is possible as it has a stable internet connection.

5. The amazing thing about Firebase products such as Cloud Firestore is that it works great with authentication, authorization, and Cloud Functions.

So, in conclusion, the newer system offers more scalability, maintainability, and power for your application. At the time of writing this book, the Firebase Cloud FireStore is in beta and may provide a very dependable future for Firebase Data Manager.

Index

www.ingramcontent.com/pod-product-compliance
Lightning Source LLC
Chambersburg PA
CBHW080630060326
40690CB00021B/4881